FIRST WORLD WAR BRITAIN

1914–1919

Peter Doyle

D0182668

SHIRE LIVING HISTORIES

How we worked • How we played • How we lived

Published in Great Britain in 2012 by Shire Publications Ltd,
Midland House, West Way, Botley, Oxford OX2 0PH,
United Kingdom.
44-02 23rd Street, Suite 219, Long Island City, NY11101,
USA.

E-mail: shire@shirebooks.co.uk www.shirebooks.co.uk

A CIP catalogue record for this book is available from the
British Library.

Shire Living Histories no. 14. ISBN-13: 978 0 74781 098 8

Peter Doyle has asserted his rights under the Copyright,
Designs and Patents Act, 1988, to be identified as the
author of this book.

Designed by Myriam Bell Design, UK and typeset in
Perpetua and Gill Sans.

Printed in China through Worldprint Ltd.

12 13 14 15 16   10 9 8 7 6 5 4 3 2 1

COVER IMAGE
A mother wishes farewell to her son as he departs to rejoin
his regiment after a period of leave at home during the
First World War. (Q30403, Imperial War Museum
Photograph Archive Collection)

ACKNOWLEDGEMENTS
All images, other than that on the cover, are from my own
collection, though I am grateful for the help of Bella
Bennett, Mark and Jan Byng, Libby Simpson and Jane Staff
in sourcing original items for me. Julie and James are my
constant support.

Shire Publications is supporting the Woodland Trust, the UK's leading woodland conservation charity, by funding the dedication of trees.

CONTENTS

"BE HONEST WITH YOURSELF. BE CERTAIN THAT YOUR SO-CALLED REASON IS NOT A SELFISH EXCUSE"

LORD KITCHENER

ENLIST TO-DAY

PREFACE

Poppies, mud, shrapnel, heavy green clouds of gas, tangled wire, unbearable noise and twisted, torn, wrecked bodies: unmistakeable images that conjure up the Western Front, 1914–18, to all of us. Almost a century on, the nightmare of the war remains vivid in our imaginations.

Soldiers returning home from the trenches, on leave or invalided out of the army, found themselves in a world that had little understanding of what they had lived through. Many struggled to adjust to 'normality'.

Yet the war could not have been fought without a huge effort back home, and the needs of the first 'total war' brought radical change to many aspects of life in Britain. As young men went abroad en masse to fight and die, their jobs had to be filled, taxes and all kinds of charitable efforts had to be raised, extraordinary demands for supplies and materiel had to be fulfilled, morale had to be maintained and somehow, family life had to go on. Meanwhile, the country that had a proud record of not having been threatened by war or invasion for a century suffered a new threat – aerial bombardment from the German zeppelins – while U-boat attacks meant that imports were cut, shortages loomed and prices, especially food prices, soared. The effects were not so dramatic as those at the Front, but they were just as profound.

The legacy of the revolutionary changes in the power of government to determine the economy lives with us still, as do the licensing laws which restricted opening hours at pubs and were inteneded to boost productivity. Many charitable activities were developed during the war, not to mention medical advances including the beginnings of plastic surgery and the beginnings of modern psychology.

The well-known military historian Peter Doyle provides a ideal guide to those troubling times, investigating the effects of war on family life, work, entertainment, education and many other dimensions in a rounded, brilliantly illustrated survey of the war years.

Peter Furtado
Series Editor

Opposite:
Typical output of the Parliamentary Recruiting Committee. Such posters played heavily upon the conscience of men not in uniform.

PROGRAMME
OF
HIS MAJESTY'S
ARMY BANDS

BRITAIN IN THE
FIRST WORLD WAR

B RITAIN had undergone many changes in the years before the start of the Great War (as the First World War was known at the time, and as it is coming to be known again). By late Victorian times, the United Kingdom of Great Britain and Ireland had extended its reach across the globe. As every schoolchild knew, the sun was never likely to set on the British Empire, its red splash depicted on maps across five continents signifying British territories that extended into hemispheres north and south, east and west. With India the jewel in the crown of the Empire, and possessions and colonies far and wide, the imperial city of London had become a truly global city. Britain was at the height of its influence.

With the ascent of Edward VII to the throne in 1901, there was a distinct change in atmosphere. Though society still had the rigid class structure so evident during the reign of Victoria, the Edwardian era was an interval of positivity, with a 'playboy' king leading a fashionable upper-class elite. There were changes for the lower classes too; the new Liberal government of 1906 swept away old laissez-faire attitudes to welfare, summoning changes that would see the birth of an incipient welfare state. This atmosphere would continue through to the eve of the Great War; and perhaps because of this (even with King George V coming to the throne in 1910), it is usual to consider the Edwardian era as extending to the outbreak of world war.

If the late Edwardian, pre-war, period was marked by the consolidation of Britain's global influence, it was also marked by a consideration of its relations within wider Europe. Hitherto typically isolationist, and dependent upon its navy for defence, Britain had been aloof from European politics for decades. Yet with Queen Victoria's wider family being distinctly European in character (the marriages of her nine children tying them into royal elites from Russia and Germany to Norway, from Romania to Spain), it is not surprising that Edward's association with the fashionable elite of European society

Opposite:
The 'Edwardian Summer': metaphor for the end of an era in August 1914. Britain carries on as normal at Southend-on-Sea in the last month of peace before the first of war.

7

The British Empire – a splash of red across the map – and its enemies, 1914.

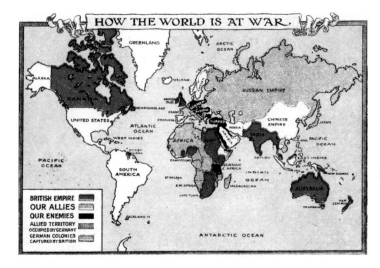

Three super-dreadnoughts. The British navy was seen as the primary strength of Britain, its main defence.

would help build bonds and alliances. In a last major act of international diplomacy by a British monarch, the king would be a driving force in the development of the Entente Cordiale between Britain and France in 1904 (and a Triple Entente between Britain, France and Russia in 1907), a bond of friendship that would have a significant impact on Britain's direction in war just ten years later. It would also be significant in terms of Britain's relationship with another neighbour – Germany.

Though close links with Germany had been mooted in the early years of the king's reign (with Edward's sister, Princess Victoria, being the empress of Germany until her death in 1901, and mother of Kaiser Wilhelm II), Edward had turned his back on the idea of a triple alliance of the three major European nations. Kaiser Wilhelm II was a cousin of King George V but there was little in the way of family warmth expressed in his direction. The kaiser was just a little too fond of grand titles and fancy uniforms for the conservative British. Instead, the British press was generally antagonistic towards Germany, with depictions of stereotypical swaggering, sabre-rattling, Prussian militarists. Suspicious also of German intentions, the British government took particular exception to the developing arms race created by the kaiser's desire to build an effective navy. This was a distinct warning shot across the bows, a growing threat to British supremacy of the seas that could not be left unchallenged. Within this atmosphere there was much scaremongering over possible German invasion plans, and much antagonism directed across the channel by the new British tabloid press. With William Le Queux's fictional tale, *The Invasion of 1910*, serialised in *The Daily Mail*, the die was cast for future war, the expectation of its coming strong.

Wartime bunting featuring the flags of the Triple Entente (Britain, France, Russia), and the country it was defending – Belgium.

Even with the growing uncertainty of global relations, the Edwardian period is associated with swagger. In this period many of Britain's civic town halls were built in a style known as 'Edwardian Baroque', borrowing heavily from the style of Sir Christopher Wren. These civic buildings were erected across the Empire signifying Britain's confidence as a global power. A leading proponent of this was Sir Edwin Lutyens, destined to be architect of New Delhi (1912–30) and ultimately of the Cenotaph in London (1920). This 'grand style' was transmitted in other ways too; the rapid growth of the rival steam-ship companies Cunard and P&O saw the creation of a succession of still larger and more luxurious trans-Atlantic steamships – the *Mauretania* and the *Titanic* being the most famous – that would become associated with the opulence of the period, as well as a metaphor for the ultimately doomed positivity of the period, with the

Germany ridiculed. Presented as brutish and stupid from before the war, the actions of its troops in Belgium in 1914 did not convince otherwise. Kaiser and son ('Big and Little Willie') would be particularly vilified.

Liver & Cunard Buildings & Dock Offices, Liverpool. No. 7.

Titanic famously sinking on its maiden voyage in April 1912. Culturally, the Edwardian, era was a rich one, with distinct movements in art, architecture and music, the time of Elgar and Vaughan Williams. But it was also the 'heroic age' of Polar, particularly Antarctic, exploration – in which Britain played a significant part. Captain Robert Scott famously lost his life on the Polar plateau

Above: Edwardian Baroque – the waterfront at Liverpool with the Royal Liver Building (1911; left) and the Port of Liverpool building (1907; right). Both illustrate the 'swagger' of the time.

in 1912, while Ernest Shackleton became stranded on the Antarctic continent in the early years of the war, not knowing its outcome. (The importance of Shackleton's expedition to national pride was such that, on the eve of war, the king had urged him to go ahead – his men would serve on the high seas and in Flanders on their return.) For children growing up in this period, both Scott and Shackleton were national heroes – cementing the British ideal of quiet, understated heroism.

Politically, there were great changes afoot. Vexing the government was the long-standing issue of Ireland, with both strong support and strong opposition in the country to the concept of Home Rule. With the opposing factions under Irish MPs John Redmond and Sir Edward Carson squaring up to each other, the Third Irish Home Rule Bill of 1914 was shelved on the eve of war. With civil war effectively stalled, the two opposing factions would instead guarantee support for Britain's war effort, its men fighting side-by-side at Messines in 1917. But not everyone would be quiet; Sir Roger Casement's doomed attempt at insurrection in 1915 – using German arms – and the more successful Irish Rebellion of 1916 would follow. The British reaction

The spirit of Edwardian Britain – Sir Ernest Shackleton as a polar explorer. On the eve of war, Shackleton would offer the services of his Antarctic expedition crew to the nation. The king urged him to continue with his expedition.

to these events was a strong one, the leaders executed.

While the question of Irish Home Rule was exercising the minds of MPs, so too were the increasingly militant activities of the Women's Social and Political Union (WSPU), otherwise known as the 'suffragettes', a movement founded by Emmeline Pankhurst in 1903. Committed to action that would bring the question of women's suffrage to public attention, the WSPU challenged authority, demanding and gaining militant actions from its members. Windows and mailboxes were attacked, fires started and other increasingly defiant acts carried out, including one that led to the death of activist Emily Davison, trampled while trying to drape a suffragette banner over the king's horse at the Epsom Derby in June 1913. Asquith's Liberal government responded with callous brutality. Like many other major political questions, all would be put on hold at the eruption of war in 1914; the first steps to universal suffrage would have to wait until 1918.

Gedenkblatt

zur Erinnerung an Seine
k.u.k. Hoheit den durchlauchtigsten
Herrn Erzherzog-Thronfolger

Franz Ferdinand

und Höchstseine Gemahlin, die
durchlauchtige Frau Herzogin

Sophie von Hohenberg

† 28. Juni 1914

Der Wiener Schuljugend gewidmet vom
Gemeinderate der k. k. Reichshaupt-
und Residenzstadt Wien

Memorial pamphlet to Franz Ferdinand, assassinated in Sarajevo, 28 June 1914. This act would precipitate the outbreak of war.

The framework of British society remained stable during this period; but perhaps some of the most significant social and economic changes to British lives were to come about during the First World War. The high point of the 'Edwardian Summer' was the August bank-holiday weekend of 1914. When Archduke Franz Ferdinand, heir to the Austro-Hungarian throne, had been assassinated in Sarajevo on 28 June 1914, the world had been thrown into turmoil. And with Austria's ally Germany poised to enact its plan to dispatch France before taking on Russia, the hope that Britain could remain aloof from European affairs was faint indeed. The people of Britain would emerge from their extended break at war, Germany having violated Belgian neutrality, and nothing would be the same again.

FAMILY LIFE

FAMILY LIFE was to be severely challenged by the Great War. With mass recruitment in the early part of the war came the possibility of the loss of husbands, fathers, and sons. Though Edwardian society in the era that preceded the war is seen as more progressive than that which had come before, family values were still strongly stratified, with relatively few women working, and men the primary breadwinners. Despite their responsibilities, many men joined up in the first months of war believing in its just cause; many others would be persuaded, and still more emotionally blackmailed. Such peer pressures saw many a man join the colours without due regard to the inevitable consequences for his family if he were killed, maimed, or otherwise rendered incapable of work.

The government recognised that married men of recruiting age might need financial inducement to leave their families: separation allowances for an average married private were paid at a weekly rate of 12s 6d for a wife alone, 17s 6d for a wife and one child, 21s for a wife and two children, and so on; but this included a compulsory 'allotment' of money from the soldier's own wages – of 6d a day (half the basic shilling a day earned by privates without other enhancements). Any other 'dependant' of the soldier, that is, 'any person who is found as a fact to have been dependant on the soldier ... to whom the soldier is bound by some natural tie...', would also need help. In such cases, the government pledged to make up the amount lost to the dependant by the soldier

Opposite: A wartime family. This soldier has been wounded twice.

Below: Separation allowances for soldiers and their families; the government hoped they would provide leverage to gain recruits.

13

Wounded soldiers would receive a war pension although this would not be generous. Papers issued to a soldier discharged from active service.

having joined the army – after the appropriate deductions, of course. How important these factors were in influencing soldiers to join up is a moot point. For many middle-class men, further enticement might have been the opportunity to return to a good job with a decent employer after the war. Some employers went out of their way to support their employee recruits; not only would their positions be held open, but they would also receive other benefits such as support of the family in some way, or the periodic sending of 'comforts' to them on the front line. For those injured in the war, and for the wives of soldiers killed in the war, there would be pensions. These would not

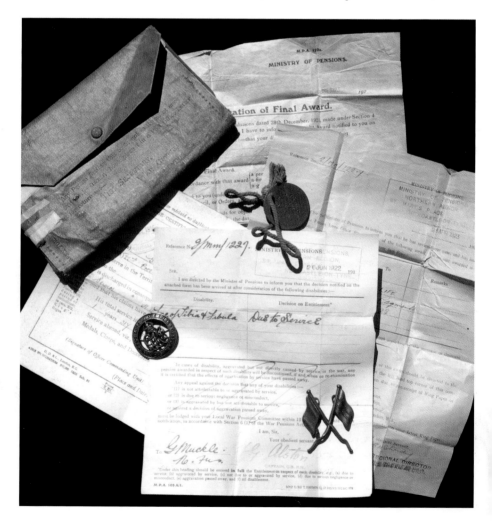

Treasury bank note (known as a 'Bradbury'), issued in 1914 in lieu of gold sovereigns.

be generous. Some 2,414,000 men were to be entitled to a war pension, the maximum they could hope to receive being 25s a week.

Though there was some economic security associated with the stability of the government's policies, this was soon to be thrown into turmoil during the Great War. With the global financial institutions in chaos at the outbreak of war, the Bank of England was forced to issue bank notes instead of sovereigns in order to safeguard gold stocks. While the notes could be exchanged at the bank for actual gold, this left a very real possibility that investors would want to recover their deposits, leaving the country's securities financially weakened. With Monday 3 August a bank holiday, the government extended the break to Friday 7 August, thereby preventing the public from forcing a run on the banks. The Treasury itself issued notes in denominations of ten shillings and one pound on Friday 7 August, and made numerous exhortations in the press to dissuade those with money to withdraw it needlessly. The pound note was here to stay.

War savings certificates and stamps. People were urged to bolster the war effort by investing their savings.

Prosecuting a world war was costly, and ensuring that there were sufficient funds in the coffers led the government to appeal for war savings from the public. Late in the war, the purchase of national war bonds and war savings certificates was portrayed as a patriotic duty, allowing the money to be used in the development and construction of the materiel of war. Many novel approaches

THE TANK BANK, "NELSON."

The Tank Bank. War-scarred tanks toured the country in 1917–18 to raise war savings.

were in promoting war savings, none more so than the 'Tank Banks' which toured Britain in 1917–18 to raise money and support from the sale of war bonds and war savings certificates. With the war's end, those boroughs that had raised the most money received a full-sized tank from the War Savings Committee, usually displayed in parks and squares. Of the 264 tanks presented, the last survivor stands in Ashford, Kent.

The cost of the war was estimated at £1 million a day in 1914, but by its end this increased to around £5.7 million pounds. While the principal financial burden would mantle those that came after in the 'brave new' post-war world; during the war spiralling costs on the home front had to be met, balanced in part by the new sources of income available to women and children as war workers. With this financial freedom came greater possibilities for working-class people; more food on the table meant health improvements and increased life expectancy. There was also some disposable income, and for once, poorer people in work could look towards purchasing 'luxuries', clothing, shoes, and so on. Yet, with the tangible benefits, there were costs. With men away from home at the front, or spending long hours at the factory, there was a strain on family life, and with mothers and children also working, there would be increased pressure on fragile relationships.

These relationships were still built on Victorian values. Within a rigid class structure, people were restrained in their domestic life. Sexual promiscuity was frowned upon, especially in unmarried women, and it was still

I was fairly taken off my feet when he came home!

— D. TEMPEST —

Home leave was a rarity for most soldiers – once a year at most.

Wartime marriage. There was a surge in marriages in 1915 – and divorces in 1919. Many new spouses would be bereaved.

common in the upper echelons for courting couples to be chaperoned. With the coming of war came the pushing of the boundaries of acceptability. Young women of the upper classes would no longer require a chaperone; and many others were to become independent wage-earners in their own right, the war having brought them out from under the shadow cast by the male domination of society. With this freedom, women were to exert their will against the strictures of Edwardian acceptability, and would now openly accompany their men friends to the darkened cinema, to the musical theatre, and to the bar. Their clothing had changed; hemlines had risen, the previously unheard-of fashion of wearing trousers or breeches commonplace. It would be difficult for former conventions to be reapplied. Some of the perceived 'excesses' were policed by women themselves when Women Police Volunteers were established in 1914. Patrolling streets and parks, the primary aim of the force was to steer young women away from unwise liaisons, to clamp down on juvenile delinquency, and to deter prostitutes from working.

For unmarried women, relationships with the heroes of the day were emotionally charged. The incidence of children born out of wedlock was to rise, but not until 1916. Prior to this, in 1915, the numbers were low; but then the number of marriages, perhaps hastily contrived, was high (with the immediate post-war divorce rate triple the pre-war rate). In both cases, this could be seen as a very natural response to the casualty lists that were routinely published in every newspaper, and to the fact that it was difficult to judge when a soldier might be next home on leave – particularly as the average soldier might only be allowed home once a year. Dr Marie Stopes's influential book, *Married Love* (published April 1918) stated: 'More than ever to-day are happy homes needed. It is my hope that this book may serve the State by adding to their number'. There was a greater awareness of sex, certainly; there were newly found freedoms from working in factories and on the land, and contraception became relatively common.

With home leave often a distant possibility, letters to and from the front took on the greatest significance, and the Army Post Office was to perform miracles in keeping loved ones in touch with each other. Letters, postcards, parcels – all were delivered to and from the fronts. But for most families, the greatest fear was the arrival of a telegram from the War Office. A stark message informing a wife or mother that her man had been killed would end: 'The War Office expresses its deepest sympathy'. In other cases, families would find that their loved one had been killed only with the return of a letter, brutally stamped 'deceased' or 'killed in action'. Mourning became a way of life.

Demobilisation was available for some men from the end of November 1918, but many more would have to wait some time for their 'ticket'. Tradesmen deemed vital for the rebuilding of Britain's peacetime industry were released first, the rest following, with around 2,750,000 men demobbed by August 1919, although the process would not be complete until 1922. Allowed to keep their greatcoat and boots, and often their uniform as well, soldiers were also issued either with an allowance for new clothes or a 'demob' suit. Old soldiers had little to show for their efforts. The campaign medals of the Great War were at best a simple star and two medals; in the hard times of the 1920s and 1930s, old soldiers down on their luck would find these hard-won items difficult to pawn.

In all, at least 10–15 per cent of those who joined up were killed – up to twice that proportion for men from Scotland. The Scots were not the only group to lose heavily; a disproportionate number – again almost a quarter – of serving middle-class men died. Large numbers of these men joined the colours in the early years, and many would serve as officers, and proportionally more officers were lost than ordinary soldiers. This would become the 'Lost Generation' that would be much discussed in post-war years, the flower of British youth. For the next of kin of those who had given their lives in the war there would be a plaque that resembled an oversized penny – earning it the nickname the 'death' or 'dead-man's' penny – some 1,150,000 plaques were produced. Many more who served would be seriously wounded, maimed or psychologically damaged – for these men, adjusting back to family life after the war would be a struggle.

The War Office telegram was feared by most families. At best it would announce capture or wounding (in this case, both) – at worst, death.

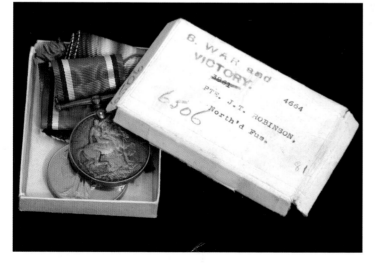

The typical medals of a Great War soldier, nicknamed 'Mutt and Jeff' (or 'Pip, Squeak and Wilfred' where there were three). Like these, many would remain unworn by their recipients.

HOME AND
NEIGHBOURHOOD

BRITAIN WAS BOOMING in the pre-war period, its population increasing; and with an aging stock of houses in its industrial heartlands that dated from the Victorian era, it was not surprising that the aspiration of the workers for better housing was increasing. The United Kingdom then encompassed the whole of Ireland (not to be independent for another ten years or so), and was markedly urbanised, with its forty-five million people concentrated, in industrial England at least, in several major conurbations. With London comprising a metropolis of four and a half million people – and a wider 'Greater' London population of at least three million more – the industrial heart of Britain, the heart of the Empire, was in the north and north-west, and the Midlands. The cities of Glasgow, Liverpool and Manchester could each boast in excess of 700,000 people, with Birmingham and Leeds around 500,000.

Of Britain's population, the majority, 80 per cent according to some estimates, were 'working class', with a middle class of around 15 per cent. Just 22 per cent of the population was rural in character, with middle-class farmers in the minority and tenant farm workers and the like the majority. The wage for a skilled worker in an industrial job was about £75 per year – a figure way below the income-tax threshold of £160 per year, unattainable earnings for most. A typical upper-middle-class salary might be twice this threshold. In all, just one and a half million people earned sufficient to qualify them as income-tax payers, a tiny proportion of the population. Contemporary estimates suggest that 16 per cent of the population lived in poverty.

For most, the housing stock available during the Great War was largely that which had been built at the end of the nineteenth century. For the working majority this meant terraced houses (or tenement buildings) with external toilets and cramped back yards. At the outbreak of war there was already a chronic housing shortage, with a

Opposite: A typical, well-constructed Edwardian house in a suburb. However, most people lived in Victorian housing, often of a much lower standard.

Late Victorian housing and tenement buildings in the Hayles Estate, Lambeth, London. Built by a charitable institution in this case, inner-city housing could be a lot less pleasant.

shortage of around 100,000–120,000 houses in urban centres; more and more families were forced to share accommodation with others – increasing by up to 20 per cent by the end of the war. With the Liberal government agenda of 1906 came the improvement of housing and circumstances. Poorer families could aspire to terraced housing with at least four rooms – though this was difficult to achieve given the housing shortage. In Glasgow, with its tradition of tenement houses, families regularly squeezed into apartments with two rooms – one a kitchen that also functioned as living room and bedroom, the other being kept as a 'front room parlour'. With just one in ten owning their houses, the arrival of the rent collector (or 'Factor') was to be a major issue, especially with rents increasing by at least 125 per cent during the war. In Clydeside, where moonlight 'flitting' to avoid payment was common, there were also rent strikes against profiteering by private landlords; the Rents and Mortgage Interest (Rent Restriction) Act of 1915 was an attempt to rule out some of the worst practices.

If the inner-city housing stock was solidly Victorian, the years leading up to the outbreak of war saw the development of suburbs – and the creation of special 'garden estates' designed to improve the lot of the workers of industrial concerns such as Lever Brothers at Port Sunlight, and Cadbury with its model village at Bournville. The development of the suburb during this period is a factor of the growth of an urban middle class – a consequence of the industrial might of Britain. While the working class was toiling in the heat of the factories, shipyards and coal mines, this burgeoning group grew to provide ancillary support, demanding a better standard of accommodation, and possessing the purchasing power to support their desires. This building phase continued well into the First World War, with 150,000 houses built a year. Yet housing shortages would become acute in post-war Britain – Lloyd George's promise of 'homes fit for heroes to live in' was stretched, requiring financial help from government under the Housing Act of 1919.

Heating and light for homes were always questions of social position and spending power. For most, heating was through coal, and lighting through gas (though electricity was becoming more common); and with coal a significant munition of war – used in manufacturing, energy production, fuelling the transport sinews of Britain through its rail system, and driving the battle fleet – there was precious little left over for the public. In 1915, the shortages starting to bite hard, concerns were high that there had been hoarding, with the inevitable charge of war profiteering by suppliers. The cost of a ton of coal was between 35 and 40 shillings – up from 28s 6d in peacetime, and the prices rose steadily. Economy was demanded,

Workers' housing at Port Sunlight, constructed in the years before the war by Lord Lever. With 150 houses per acre typical in some inner-city areas, Lever insisted that he would build 13.5 houses in the same space, to a high specification. Lever would employ some of the best architects in the country to build the village.

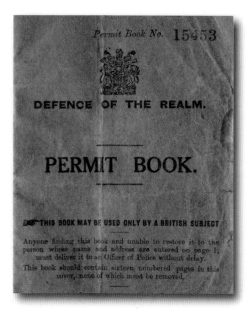

Civilians working in military installations would have to carry identification booklets like this following the introduction of the Defence of the Realm Act, 1914. DORA was to control the movement of people across the country.

'rations' limited to 2 cwt for a small house in 1917–18; the coal queue became a familiar sight on the streets of Britain. People fortunate enough to live in a coal-producing area scoured beaches and pits for abandoned lumps of the precious black mineral.

One of the most far-reaching impacts of the war was the introduction of the Defence of the Realm Act – universally known as DORA. First passed as law on 8 August 1914, it was to control the British public in ways never seen before. Though the act itself was originally short and to the point, DORA was revised and extended at least four times during the war, giving the government greater and greater means of imposing the needs of total war on the population. Originally drafted as a means of protecting sensitive installations and public works from possible sabotage, DORA would eventually control the lives of ordinary people, restricting their movements, their social habits and their working life. Under the act, civilians could be tried by courts martial, arrested by the military and treated as if subject to military law – though this was later amended, giving suspects the right to demand trial. DORA laid down strict rules regarding communication with or assisting the enemy, spreading rumours or false reports likely to hinder the military, or spreading disaffection.

The act also allowed the government to requisition land or vital factories. DORA gave provisions for the control of a great many other, largely unconnected, aspects of life; aspects that impinged upon the protection of the nation. Through DORA came lighting restrictions – first applied in London on 11 September 1914 – and the introduction of British Summer Time, intended to extend the daylight hours for farmers. In 1918, continuing fuel shortages meant that British Summer Time was extended, and there was even a fuel-saving curfew order, made by the president of the Board of Trade, ordering shops, places of entertainment and other public places to extinguish lights by 10.30 p.m.

While the Great War was a conflict like no other, no one had expected to see death and destruction dealt on the streets of Britain. Yet German intentions were expressed clearly in Ernst Lissauer's 1914 poem *Hassgesang gegen England* – otherwise known as the 'Hymn of

Hate': 'We love as one, we hate as one, We have one foe and one alone
– England!' *'Gott Strafe England!'* (God punish England!) became a
popular slogan in Germany, though much lampooned in Britain. For
the first time for centuries, the British public would be under grave
threat from land, sea and air.

One of the immediate causes of the Great War was the rapid growth
of the kaiser's pet plan – his attempt to expand the Imperial German
Navy. At the outset of war, with the British navy dispersed to tackle its
commitments, the more concentrated Imperial German Navy sought
opportunities to trap small numbers of British ships and destroy them.
With this in mind, Admiral Hipper planned raids on the British coast
that he hoped would bring him success, the British navy surely having
to respond by sending ships to the beleaguered home coast. The first
of these raids, at Great Yarmouth on 3 November 1914, was a failure.
A more ambitious raid, targeting Scarborough and Hartlepool, was
planned for 16 December 1914. At 8.00 a.m., German ships shelled
Scarborough, hitting the Grand Hotel, churches and private properties;
the nearby town of Whitby was also hit. Hartlepool was assaulted ten
minutes later; over a thousand shells were hurled at the town,
damaging factories, homes and churches. Eighty-six civilians and seven
soldiers were killed, 438 were injured. The raids were a propaganda
victory for the British – 'Remember Scarborough' now replaced
'Remember Belgium' on recruiting posters.

The assault on Britain was not limited to bombardment from
ships, however, and the next phase would be the use of airships –
Zeppelins. The first aerial attacks were approved by the kaiser himself
in January 1915 – though at first excluding London – these would be

Raids on the
north-east towns
of Scarborough,
Whitby and
Hartlepool by
German Admiral
Hipper
in 1914 would kill
ninety-three and
injure 438. The
attack would be
a propaganda
failure for the
Germans; the
British issued
these 'iron
crosses' to
commemorate
the incident.

Zeppelin 'baby killers' – the first raids would be against the east coast of England in 1915.

Special constables were recruited to protect the public – carrying out many tasks that during the Second World War would be done by the Air Raid Precautions service. They were also the butt of jokes.

By George - a beastly bomb - what!

night raids targeting military installations on the Thames estuary. The raids soon escalated. The first successful one was on the night of 19 January, when two Zeppelins attacked East Anglia with high explosive bombs and incendiaries, killing four and injuring sixteen; it was the shape of things to come. London began to be targeted in February. Though early attempts were limited, at 11.00 p.m. on 31 May 1915, Captain Linnarz of Zeppelin LZ38 dropped the first enemy bombs – some 3,000 pounds of explosive – on the capital. Seven people were killed and thirty-five injured. The response from the ground was ineffectual, with no aircraft to meet it, no guns fired at it, no searchlights trained on it.

Raids on Britain would continue into the summer, though the short nights were a problem for the Zeppelins, which depended on the cover of darkness; and the bombing started to get heavier. Anti-aircraft defences were still ineffectual – though the pencil-like shape of the airships was often caught in searchlights, the problem was that neither anti-aircraft fire nor aircraft were able to intercept the high-flying airships. In all there were twenty raids in 1915, with 37 tons of bombs dropped at a cost of 181 dead and 455 wounded.

In the face of threats by aerial assault – as well as the periodic spy scares and anti-German riots – the government turned to an act passed in 1831, allowing the recruitment of special constables. Unpaid volunteers, special constables at first wore only civilian clothes augmented by a duty armband and decorated truncheon; but from 1916 they were issued with a dark-blue uniform and peaked cap. Their role was varied: guarding vulnerable points (including reservoirs against poisoning), patrolling the streets, giving warnings of air raids (and announcing their end), and assisting the public during these raids.

The clamour for a more effective active defence led to the army taking command in early 1916, deploying 271 anti-aircraft guns and 258 searchlights in the hunt for the raiders, and ten home fighter squadrons equipped with newer aircraft and with new ammunition – a mixture of explosive, incendiary and tracer bullets. The Zeppelin raids continued into 1916, with larger numbers of airships targeting London and other cities in the eastern part of the country. The largest raid was on the night of 2 September, which was to be a turning point – as on this night Lieutenant William Leefe Robinson became the first pilot to actively shoot down an airship over Britain, the rigid-bodied Schütte-Lanz SL11. Robinson fired three drums of ammunition into the airship, which quickly caught fire and was sent to earth as a fireball, the crew killed outright. The shooting down became a celebrated event and fragments of the destroyed craft were sold to aid the Red Cross. Leefe Robinson was awarded the Victoria Cross, but would later be shot down in France. He spent the rest of the war in a prison camp before tragically succumbing to the influenza pandemic at the end of the war.

Though this event finished off the German army's interest in Zeppelin attacks, the Imperial German Navy continued with them well into 1916, with twenty-three raids in total at a cost of 293 civilian lives. But the 1916 raids were marked by increasing successes for the defenders. The L32 was shot down by Second Lieutenant Frederick Sowrey on the night of 23 September. With the Zeppelin engulfed by flames, many of the crew decided to jump for it rather than be

The destruction of Schütte-Lanz SL11, by Lieutenant William Leefe Robinson on 2 September 1916, is commemorated by a stone obelisk in the village of Cuffley, Hertfordshire, which was paid for by the readers of *The Daily Express*.

The Potters Bar
Zeppelin, L31 –
destroyed with
all hands.

ZEPPELIN BROUGHT DOWN, IN FLAMES
At POTTER'S BAR, MIDNIGHT, OCTOBER 1st, 1916.
(DRAWN BY AN EYE WITNESS.)

burnt. None survived. The L33, another airship on the same raid, was
forced down intact at Little Wigborough, Essex, before being set alight
by the crew. Its sister ship, the L31, would come to a sticky end a
week later, shot down by Second Lieutenant Wulstan Tempest and
crashing with all hands at Potters Bar, Hertfordshire.

With Zeppelin attacks losing their effectiveness, Germany planned
a new phase of aerial attacks for 1917, employing large Gotha GIV

bombers in daylight. A new air unit was formed to carry out the attacks, the so-called *Englandgeschwader*, based near Ghent, in Belgium. The first attack on the capital was to be on 25 May 1917, but poor weather meant that the bombers attacked Folkestone and the army camp at Shorncliffe, causing a sharply increased number of fatalities compared with the Zeppelin phase. The first effective raid on London was also the deadliest; on 13 June 1917 there were 162 deaths including eighteen children – most of them under six years old – at an elementary school in Poplar, East London.

Further raids saw casualties mount, with the next attack, on 7 July 1917, resulting in civilian deaths from falling anti-aircraft shells (with 103 recorded falling by the London Fire Brigade); fifty-four were killed across the City of London. There would be eight daylight raids in all before improvements in air defences – with the creation of the coordinated London Air Defence Area (LADA) – caused the Germans to abandon daylight raids, presaging another war to come. Night raids commenced on 4 September 1917, the effects of the first raid evident in the blast-scarred monument of Cleopatra's Needle, on London's Embankment.

One of the most tragic raids took place on 18 January 1918, with the attack on Long Acre in Covent Garden, where a single 300-kg bomb killed thirty-eight people. The Germans pitted still larger aircraft against Britain with the 'Giant', one of which would drop a 1,000-kg bomb on Chelsea during a raid on 16 February. The raids continued until the last, and largest, of the war: on the night of 19 May 1918, thirty-eight Gothas and three Giants attacked the capital; seventy-two bombs were dropped over a wide area of London, but at a cost of six German aircraft lost to the air defences and a seventh destroyed on landing. This would spell the last of the Gotha raids, and the last attack on the mainland of Britain, until the Blitz.

Memorial to the dead children of the North Street School, Poplar, killed during the first Gotha raid on London, 13 June 1917.

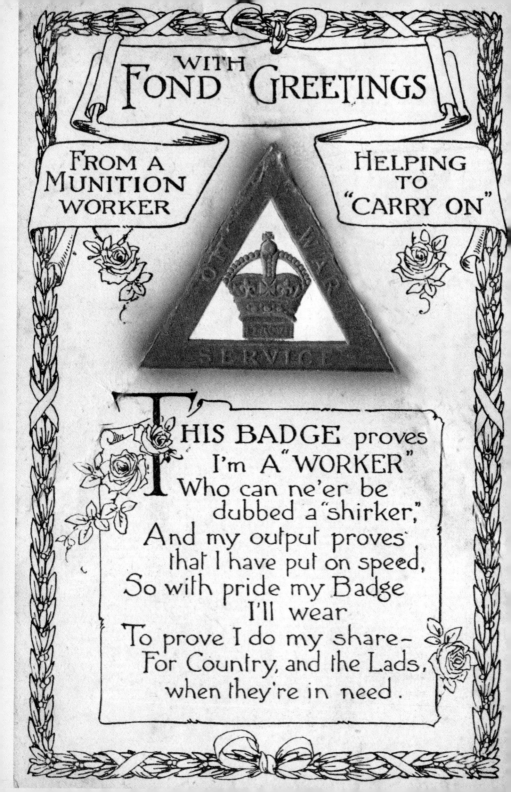

WITH
FOND GREETINGS

FROM A
MUNITION
WORKER

HELPING
TO
"CARRY ON"

ON WAR SERVICE

THIS BADGE proves
I'm A "WORKER"
Who can ne'er be
dubbed a "shirker,"
And my output proves
that I have put on speed,
So with pride my Badge
I'll wear
To prove I do my share—
For Country, and the Lads,
when they're in need.

WORK

GREAT BRITAIN had long held on to its position as the only major European power not to depend upon conscription for its armed forces. The onset of war drew many men to the colours, but it would take a lot more than this to reach the peak of recruitment seen in 1914–15. This resulted from the reporting of German atrocities (overplayed at the time but atrocities nonetheless): the summary execution of Belgian civilians, and the torching of mediaeval architectural gems. Voluntary recruitment reached its peak in August 1914, after the setbacks suffered by the British Expeditionary Force at Mons, when men felt obliged to join to 'answer their country's call'. Highly charged recruiting posters issued by the Parliamentary Recruiting Committee, and the actions of some women in handing out white feathers to those at home, all led to the pressure on the workforce.

Opposite: 'From a Munition Worker'. Women munitions workers would wear a distinctive triangular 'On War Service' badge, marked 1916 for its first year of issue.

Left: 'Lady recruiters wanted'. The original caption for this press photograph reads: 'shirkers will have a hard time in the future'.

31

Understanding that the war would be costly in manpower, the Secretary of State for War, Field Marshal Lord Kitchener, made a direct appeal to the public for more men, his image used to promote his appeal. 'Kitchener's Army' was the result. The 'First Hundred Thousand' (K1) were recruited within days of the appeal. Kitchener was to issue four

Kitchener Blue – emergency uniforms worn by the men of Kitchener's Army in lieu of khaki.

further appeals through the late summer and early autumn of 1914. Recruiting offices sprang up across the country, with local municipal buildings and mobile recruiting offices pressed into service, usually bedecked with banners and posters. Would-be soldiers were given the briefest of medicals.

Initial recruitment was steady; but following a request from the City of London to raise a whole battalion of 'stockbrokers', an avalanche of 'City' and 'Pals' battalions were formed from men with similar backgrounds and circumstances. This was in large due to the action of Lord Derby, the so-called 'King of Lancashire' and future secretary of state for war, who introduced the notion that men of the 'commercial classes' might wish to serve their country in a battalion of their comrades, their 'pals'. The 'Liverpool Pals' was the result. The implication was that middle-class men would not be forced to serve alongside men of 'lower social class' who they would neither know nor understand. The government having correctly judged the snobbery of the time, the initiative was a resounding success.

The concept spread like wildfire throughout the industrial north and Midlands. Becoming a matter of civic pride, each battalion was raised by local dignitaries, who fed, clothed and equipped the men until the unit was taken over by the War Office – the costs of raising them only then being met by the government. Recruits were more often than not clothed in civilian garb, and as training camps had not yet been formed or established, Kitchener's men found themselves still living at home. As a stopgap, simple uniforms were supplied in what has become known as Kitchener Blue – blue serge in place of khaki. Recruitment soared, reaching 1,186,357 by the end of 1914.

Yet with the initial rush of men to join the colours in the early stages of the war, it was inevitable that there would be others less keen, men who ran the risk while in civilian clothing of censure from the female vigilantes of the Order of the White Feather. Founded in 1914 by Admiral Charles Fitzgerald and the author Mary Ward, the organisation persuaded women to present men who were not in uniform with a white feather – a traditional badge of cowardice – though these men might include wounded, off-duty or on-leave soldiers and sailors. Despite these actions, recruitment took a sharp dip in 1915, declining month-on-month from its peak in August 1914.

National Registration Card. Introduced in July 1915, registration was the first step to compulsory military service.

If Britain was to preserve its role in the war, some action to stem the tide was urgently needed. Lord Derby was appointed director of recruitment in October 1915, intended to address this decline.

But the first steps to compulsion had already been taken with the National Registration Act of July 1915. The act required every citizen between the ages of fifteen and sixty-five to register their name, place of residence, nature of work and other details, and to receive a national registration card. By October 1915 there were 21,627,596 names on the register, of which 5,158,211 were men of military age. Of this figure, 1,519,432 men were identified as being in reserved occupations, vital to the war effort. Under national registration men exempted from military service became known as 'starred', from the black star that was added against their names on the official records. The engineering trades' unions had been made responsible for identifying and exempting skilled men from military service, issuing their members with trade cards. All would wear 'On War Service' badges and carry 'protection certificates' – protecting them from the white feather.

National registration identified that there were at least 3.4 million men who were technically able to join the forces; but by the autumn of 1915, the number actually joining was falling at an alarming rate, no longer sufficient to fulfil the requirement of 35,000 men per week envisaged by Lord Kitchener. Lord Derby drew up a scheme that

This Certificate must be signed by the holder in the space provided below and must be returned to the Society by which it was issued when it ceases to be in force.

Signature) of Holder) *S. G. Daniel*

Place in which Registered under National Registration Act—

Sheffield

Date *10/16*

ORIGINAL.

TRADE CARD.

No. 411774

CERTIFICATE OF EXEMPTION

ISSUED BY THE

MILITARY AUTHORITIES

On ground that holder is marked in Military Register as not to be called up for service with the Colours so long as Certificate is in force.

NOTE.—This Certificate is not granted under the Military Service Acts, 1916.

W10011—R801 203,000 11/16 HWV(M40/2) G16/1766
10311—R 64 200,000 1/17

Exemption certificate for Sydney George Daniel, a steel worker from Sheffield. He would later join the Royal Air Force in 1918.

would force the issue; either it would work, or would signal conscription. The 'Derby Scheme' entailed the voluntary attestation (a legal undertaking to join the colours when called to them) of all men between eighteen and forty, with men of the same age and marital status being grouped together to be called to the colours in batches. Married men would be last to go. Lord Derby invited all eligible men to attest by 15 December 1915; over two million of the three and a half million men available for military service failed to attest. If it was simply an experiment, it could be deemed a failure; but for Lord Derby it paved the way to compulsory service.

With the introduction of the Military Service Act of January 1916, all fit single men between the ages of eighteen and forty-one were compelled to join the colours, married men joining them in the second Military Service Act of May 1916. Unfit men were exempted for the time being; but three further acts, in April 1917, January 1918 and April 1918, would find ways of 'combing out' more men for military service (the last reducing the recruitment age to seventeen, while, at the same time, increasing it to fifty-five).

Conscientious objectors – COs or 'conchies' – were those who objected to military service due to their deep-held beliefs that war was wrong. Under the military service acts, conscientious objectors had to appear before a tribunal to have their case determined on an individual basis. Those holding the most fundamental objections refused to engage in any work, civilian or military, which might support the prosecution of the war. For these men, the alternative could be a long spell in prison 'with hard labour' for refusing to serve.

Britain was one of the most industrialised nations, its Empire built on the back of its industrial prowess. The Midlands could boast of being the workshop of the Empire, but with the need for manpower transferring to the armed forces, there was soon a crisis in employment: soldiers alone could not win a war. Skilled workers were required to help feed the guns, build the ships, and forge weapons. In the face of peer pressure to join the colours, maintaining the level of skilled workers was no mean task – especially as, in some cases, up to

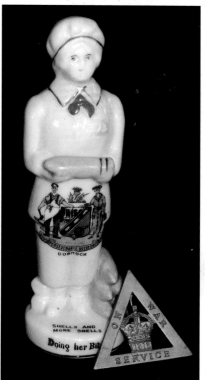

Crested china model of a female munitions worker, illustrated with a women's On War Service badge. The crest on this model is from the huge National Filling Factory at Gretna.

40 per cent of the workforce had joined up. The poverty of munitions available to the troops was to come into sharp focus during the 'shell shortage' scandal of May 1915. Lord Northcliffe's *Daily Mail* reported that the failure of Sir John French's offensive at Neuve-Chapelle in March was due to inadequate artillery preparation before battle, with few shells and a prevalence of 'duds'. The *Daily Mail* laid the blame squarely at the door of Lord Kitchener and the War Office. There was truth in the allegations; with the War Office relying on a pre-war supply system, using existing factories, simply increasing orders was not going to satisfy demand. The scandal caused the Liberal government to fall, the coalition that followed creating the Ministry of Munitions in May 1915, and appointing David Lloyd George as minister in July.

The Munitions of War Act that followed in August 1915 brought all munitions manufacturers under the control of the new ministry. By 1918, it managed directly 250 government factories, and supervised 20,000 more. There was a bewildering array of types: National Filling Factories (NFF), National Projectiles Factories (NPF), National Shell Factories (NSF), and a whole host of industrial sites concerned with the myriad aspects of trench warfare. While just 500,000 shells were produced in 1914, in 1917 some 76 million were manufactured. In all, some 2.5 million men would work in munitions factories during the war – but this would be inadequate. New sources of labour would be required, and the government turned to the unions in order to implement what would be termed 'dilution' of the skilled workforce – the use of unskilled male labour, and women.

Prior to conscription, men had been encouraged to register as 'war munitions volunteers', a status that exempted them from military service – at least in the short run – but required them to be mobile. Women war work volunteers had been sought in March 1915, yet take-up of them by the factories was slow at first. As women volunteers were viewed with some suspicion by many male workers, agreement to take women into factories had to be reached between employers and unions – the first such agreement was attained in November 1914, and was followed by a variety of others leading up to the adoption of the Munitions of War Act in 1915. With this in place, further negotiations would follow to allow women to take on more and more work in what were traditionally 'closed shops'.

With these moves, and with an increasing number of men being 'combed out' of war work in order to take their place on the front line, women would be called to the munitions factories as 'munitionettes' or 'Tommy's sisters'. With munitions including

everything from the filling of shells through to the manufacture of boots, bandages and tents, there was a crying need for labour, and an estimated female workforce of 800,000 women would be employed in all aspects of the industry, some 594,600 working under the aegis of the Ministry of Munitions. Of these, the largest proportion, almost 250,000, were engaged in the filling and manufacture of shells; the remainder helped create ordnance pieces, rifles, small-arms ammunition; they also worked with chemicals and on the myriad devices needed in trench warfare. In many cases, women would come to outnumber men. At the huge National Filling Factory at Gretna, 11,576 women were employed, comprising almost 70 per cent of the workforce; they made cordite, nitroglycerine and other explosives.

Munitions work was long and hard, but women were attracted to it for a variety of reasons, whether from patriotic duty or simply from a desire to better their lives. Most were from working-class backgrounds, but there were also others from richer backgrounds who desired the opportunity to 'do their bit' for their country. Some women were mobile, housed in YWCA hostels or lodgings, with canteens set up to cater for them, and welfare systems in place. They were reasonably well paid, typically £2 2s 4d a week; yet this was still half the wage paid to men – there would be a long way to go for equal treatment.

Munitions workers at the Royal Ordnance Factory, the Woolwich Arsenal.

Poem sold on the streets by ex-servicemen who were out of work in the harsh post-war world.

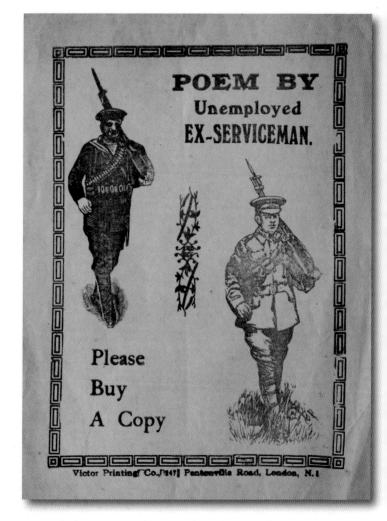

With the pressure of increased productivity demands, allegations of profiteering, and the rising price index, there was increasing unrest in the workplace from late 1915 onwards. The question of the 'dilution' of the workforce in non-war production was also a matter of some concern for some men. This unrest would boil over in strikes in the Clydeside shipbuilding factories in the winter of 1915–16, and in widespread industrial disputes during 1917. Strike action became a national bone of contention, particularly amongst many fighting men, who would presumably have been happy to give up their position in the firing line to a worker who had had the benefit of increased wages. Such opposed stances would add to the unrest; Britain had the most militant workforce of all of the combatant nations. One estimate is 3,227 strikes in the 1915–18 period, involving 2.6 million striking workers, costing the nation almost eighteen million working days.

Working in munitions factories was understandably dangerous. The manufacture and handling of chemicals, particularly trinitrotoluene (TNT), led to insidious disease, as men and women worked with little protection. Inhaling and ingesting dust led to the onset of toxic jaundice, with women experiencing yellowing of the skin and colour changes in their hair – leading to them being called 'canaries'. The condition was not to be taken lightly, however, and deaths from poisoning were a fact of life. And if poisoning was not enough, with so many explosive chemicals being handled on a day-to-day basis, it was not surprising that accidents happened. One of the first was at the gunpowder mill at Uplees, in Faversham, Kent on 2 April 1916; following a fire, the explosion, involving 200 tons of TNT, killed 105 workers. It is less well known, though, than 'London's largest explosion', which took place at Silvertown on 19 January 1917. Here, fifty tons of TNT ignited following a fire at 6.52 p.m. Some seventy-three workers killed, and the blast was sufficient to damage a substantial number of buildings in this part of East London, with thousands of people being made homeless. Yet the largest loss of life was at National Shell Filling Factory No. 6 near Chilwell in Nottinghamshire. The factory was created in the wake of the shell scandal of 1915, and the explosion there on 1 July 1918 killed 137 people, most of whom were buried in a mass grave at St Mary's Church, Attenborough. There were several other accidents: at Ashton under Lyme in 1917 (killing forty-three), and at Barnbow in Yorkshire (killing thirty-five). Smaller accidents added to the death toll; arguably munitions workers were as much on the front line as the soldiers.

It is a cliché that soldiers returned from the war in 1918–19 expecting a 'land fit for heroes to live in' – the phrase used by David Lloyd George in campaigning during the 'coupon' or 'khaki' election of December 1918. He was to remain prime minister, a post he had held since 1916, when he replaced H. H. Asquith. Yet delivering this ideal would not be easy. With so many servicemen demobilised, and in the depth of a post-war slump following the gearing of a nation for 'total war', finding employment was a nightmare task. Despite the empty promises, for many ex-servicemen the only way of scratching a living in the cold, post-war world would involve charity and selling small goods, the long struggle to find employment becoming a national disgrace.

Here's one or two valuables to show I don't forget you in these hard times!

FOOD AND DRINK

THE QUESTION OF FOOD was to become a major one during the war; with Britain so hopelessly dependent on imports (up to 60 per cent of its food stocks at the outbreak of war), it was vulnerable to attacks on its supply system. Yet early on in the Great War, food control was unheard of, and it was not until 1916 that there was a move towards some form of formal restrictions on consumption. At the outbreak of war, concerns over shortages among the middle and upper classes led to widespread hoarding. That other unholy act, 'profiteering', was also a major preoccupation of the newspapers, and the opportunity to make money from decreased supply was perhaps too great to miss for some retailers. Both actions were loudly condemned in the press, yet rationing was not enacted until 1917.

Imperial Germany was intent on starving Britain into submission, U-boats targeting any ship – neutral included – that might represent a lifeline for Britain in terms of food supply. Around 300,000 tons of shipping was sunk a month; in April 1917 alone, a record 550,000 tons of shipping was lost. This level of destruction meant that some foodstuffs were in short supply. It would also lead to a backlash against those shops bearing Germanic names, with riots and looting prevalent in 1915.

Not until December 1916 was a specific government department – the Ministry of Food – established to deal with such issues. Set up in the wake of concerns over profiteering and hoarding (rather than the effect of German submarines on imports), this body replaced the Cabinet Committee on Food Supplies that had been created early in the war to ensure that there were adequate supplies of the most important foodstuffs. The fact soon dawned that the submarine menace was a critical one, and the ministry set about persuading the nation that some restraint would be needed. A food controller (Lord

Opposite: Postcard illustrating some of the shortages or restrictions experienced by the British people: beer, sugar, potatoes – and money.

Below: Sugar bowl from 1918 – marked with the weekly sugar ration. Sugar was the first commodity to be rationed in the face of real shortages.

The sinking of the Cunard liner *Lusitania*, here depicted upon the cover of *The Daily Mirror*, would lead to anti-German riots and looting of German-owned shops in 1915.

LUSITANIA TORPEDOED BY GERMAN PIRATE

The Daily Mirror

CERTIFIED CIRCULATION LARGER THAN ANY OTHER PICTURE PAPER IN THE WORLD

No. 3,600. SATURDAY, MAY 8, 1915 16 PAGES One Halfpenny.

THE HUNS CARRY OUT THEIR THREAT TO MURDER : FAMOUS CUNARDER SUNK OFF THE IRISH COAST.

Devonport at first, then Lord Rhondda) was also appointed, to 'promote economy and maintain the food supply of the country', as well as to increase production and reduce food waste. Exports of food were prohibited, and a raft of sub-committees and commissions were charged with keeping prices down and ensuring supplies were adequate. Food prices increased steadily through the war, and gave rise to numerous re-occurring charges of profiteering. Prices of most commodities rose by 50 per cent over the period of the war, others by much more. Fresh meat would increase by some 100 per cent (imported, frozen meat almost twice this); fish by almost 200 per cent, sugar by 250 per cent and fresh eggs by 400 per cent. Some form of fair distribution system was needed.

With real demand, and little or no home-grown sources, the supply of sugar was a real problem. As much as 70 per cent of the pre-war supply had been derived from sugar beet grown in Germany and Austria, the rest coming from far-flung British colonies and dependent on a transatlantic shipping trade. With the U-boat campaign biting deep, shortages became acute. Sugar became the first commodity to be rationed on a national basis, and in July 1917 householders were issued with ration cards that entitled them to a ration of half a pound of sugar a week. Sugar was one thing, but the supply of meat was quite a different matter.

With much meat imported from the Americas, getting hold of even the cheapest cuts was difficult. Meat consumption would fall from 2.36 pounds to 1.53 pounds per person per week by the end of the war. With stocks running low, shortages began – and queues at butcher's shops and grocers started to lengthen. The War Savings Committee tried to institute 'Eat Less Meat' days in 1916 to assist; and the nation turned to fish, the inevitable demand driving prices up. Offal was another alternative. With 1917 a particularly hard year on the Western Front, and no sign of a breakthrough, people started to fear that the war would never end – and that the country would start to run out of food. Panic buying and hoarding reasserted itself, and food control committees started to examine any evidence of waste, from throwing rice at weddings to the size of the offerings in teashops. It was obvious that rationing would have to be extended.

Idealised image of a society lady serving in a canteen, 1918. Such canteens sprang up across the country – and 'canteening' was a popular way of serving the country.

In the densely populated region of London and the Home Counties, food supply was a major concern, and the London food committees were the first to ask for the rationing scheme to be expanded. Early in 1918, ten million people were the first to receive two ration cards, each entitling them to a weekly ration of meat and fats (butter and margarine). The householder was to register with a supplier, and would then be granted a ration based on cancelled coupons per week. Each retailer was guaranteed a supply, and the registered householder would have to queue outside the shop. It is estimated that

Now, Woman has been called upon
And put upon her honour,
The boys can rest assured of this –
They can rely upon her.

Bread shortages were of real concern; so much so that the king was forced to make a proclamation asking the British people to eat less bread. This postcard tries to put a cheery message to it.

around one and a quarter million people queued each week outside shops for their ration. To guarantee supply, just as a customer was tied to a retailer, so the retailer was tied to a wholesaler, and the wholesaler to the importer – assuming that the ships could make it through. In addition, the government set up a system of National Kitchens in June 1918, supplying a range of simple but wholesome foods – and decreasing waste through catering en masse. For some upper-class women intent on 'doing their bit', working in such establishments, or 'canteening', became a craze.

Bread was an important food reserve for much of the population – it was processed, already cooked and cheap. Attempts to increase the yield of wheat from British farms were reasonably successful, yet with the submarine threat to the supply of wheat from overseas, baking sufficient bread to meet demand was a challenging task. Appeals were made to 'eat less bread' to conserve stocks, with campaigns and propaganda to boot; this was easily asked for, but poorer families found this self-sacrifice a difficult task. In early May 1917 the king issued a royal proclamation: 'We, being persuaded that the abstention from all unnecessary consumption of grain will furnish the surest and most effectual means of defeating the devices of Our enemies... We do for this purpose more particularly exhort and charge all heads of households to reduce the consumption of bread in their respective families by at least one-fourth...' For some families, this was easier said than done.

The cost of bread became a major concern: an average price for a loaf was around 6d in 1914, by June 1917 it had risen to over 11d. In October 1917 the government felt it necessary to subsidise the humble loaf, fixing the price at 9d, a subsidy that was to cost the nation an estimated £40 million. Though bread was never subject to rationing, its texture was to suffer markedly. Substituting the wheat were a whole variety of suspect ingredients – from potato flour to chalk. These were intended to bulk up the mix, but instead managed to create a universally detested loaf that was 'dark in colour, rough in texture and often unpleasant in flavour'. The other staple, the potato, was similarly in short supply. There was a serious shortage of the root vegetable in 1917, and this meant that the supply of seed potatoes was put at risk for 1918. To avert disaster the food controller distributed

OUT FOR VICTORY.

THE ALLOTMENT HOLDER.

Too old to fight, but doing his bit to beat the U boats.

Under the Defence of the Realm Act (DORA), underused land was turned into allotments. Seed potatoes granted to allotment holders helped alleviate shortages in 1918. This postcard, from the National War Savings Committee, celebrates the process.

some 15,000 tons of seed potatoes, many of them to allotment holders. Under DORA, many unused land areas were commandeered and converted into allotments, thereby increasing the harvestable area of Britain to the extent that by the summer of 1918 there were 100,000 acres of allotments available for growing food in England and Wales. The seed potatoes came good, and large crops were raised that helped avert the feared shortage.

Women's Land Army (WLA) distinctive green armband, worn by all members with their uniform of breeches, overall and hat.

For both wheat and potatoes there was an obvious need for sufficient workers so that the harvest could be quickly and efficiently brought in. This became particularly acute in 1918, when the manpower shortage on the Western Front meant that around 30,000 men who would normally have been exempted from military service to work on the land were now suddenly conscripted. Lloyd George looked for help, and appeals were made for volunteers to take a hand in bringing the harvest home: 'Every woman who has the great gifts of youth and strength, if not already devoting these to essential work for her country, should resolve to do so today. If she lives in a village, let her go out and work in the fields from her home. If she can give her whole time let her join the ranks of the Land Army... I know this appeal will be heard.'

National ration books, 1918. Replacing the earlier cards, these books contained coupons.

The Women's Land Army (WLA) was formed in 1917, though women volunteers started to appear on British farms from 1915 onwards, members of organisations such as the Women's National Land Service Corps and the Women's Defence Relief Corps. The importance of working the land to feed the people of Britain was well understood – but there was a growing resentment in some quarters about the influence of gentlemen farmers in retaining male workers as 'starred men', exempt from enlistment. With conscription, more and more

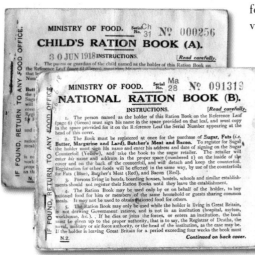

men were 'combed out' from such situations. Women would be needed, with those over eighteen invited to volunteer to assist local farmers. After six weeks of training they were employed in milking, care of animals and general work in the fields. Paid initially at a rate of 18s a week, this rose to 20s once efficiency tests had been passed. The Land Army women were issued with a free uniform of boots, breeches, jersey, hat and overalls – worn with a distinctive bright-green armband upon which was a red crown. Though some ardent male traditionalist farmers resisted the change, the Board of Agriculture and Board of Trade mounted successful campaigns to promote the WLA, such that by 1918 it numbered some 20,000 members, with a larger estimate of a quarter of a million women otherwise working the land as labourers. The work was hard – but necessary if Britain was to survive.

The quality of wartime food was variable – and cheaper margarine was to become universally disliked – but the rationing system worked. So well did it work that it was extended to the rest of the country from April 1918, with simplified national ration books issued to cover all rationed commodities: sugar, fats (butter, margarine, lard), butcher's meat and bacon. This time there were detachable coupons, yellow for sugar, blue for fats and red for meat and bacon. Spare coupons were included in case new items were rationed; jam was taken into the system in November – but new coupons were added to the books at this point. The ration worked out, per person, per week as: approximately 1 pound of uncooked (butcher's) meat (the ration was worked out in prices, not weight, fixed as far as possible to match a national standard and food value); 6 ounces of butter and/or margarine and 2 ounces of lard; 4–8 ounces of bacon and/or ham depending on the district; 8 ounces of sugar; 1.5 ounces of cheese and 1.5 ounces of tea. Rationing would stagger on until 1920, with meat off ration in December 1919, butter by May 1920, and sugar by the end of that year.

Bovril and Oxo were popular brands of proprietary meat extracts during the war. This advert dates from 1917.

WOMAN'S LIFE

ONE PENNY,   No. 288 (New Series).   AUGUST 11, 1917.

Free Coupon Pattern—LITTLE GIRL'S JUMPER FRO

SHOPPING AND STYLE

MEN'S CLOTHING OF THE PERIOD was conservative, and with Edwardian times being predominantly class structured, the clothing worn reflected social class. Gradually, civilian clothes would give way to military and naval uniforms. However, photographs showing the recruitment crazes of 1914 at the recruiting offices reveal a mingling of all social classes, with everyone clad typically in three-piece suits, and topped off with a hat of some kind. Waistcoats were common to all, and jacket lapels were fastened quite high, rather than displaying much of the shirt and waistcoat. Hardwearing and well-cleated boots were worn by most.

Opposite:
Woman's Life, a woman's interest magazine from 1917; large hats were still in vogue.

A typical 'knut', the man about town, with cane, gloves and boater. Such men would be the target of women distributing white feathers.

In general terms, men of working-class background were more likely to be clad in rather more shapeless suits than those from middle-class backgrounds. Suits were worn on all occasions, from the workplace to the pub. Large flat caps were usually worn, sometimes of incredible dimensions; it was rare for a man to be seen without a hat. Middle-class suits were better cut, with slimmer lines, and closer-fitting trousers tapering to turn-ups, usually worn with well-polished shoes. This is the classic image of the well-to-do young 'knut' – a gadabout, a person often accused of being a shirker. The term 'knut' was personified in the 1914 hit song: 'I'm Gilbert the Filbert, the knut with a k.   The pride of Piccadilly, the blasé roué'. Such men would wear shirts with high, detachable collars with rounded edges and ties. Waistcoats would be worn with Albert chains and pocket watches, often adorned by fobs. Wristwatches were less common in pre-war times, and were considered effeminate; yet during the war they became a phenomenon, with 'wristlets' being worn by officers and men alike.

Hats worn by the middle classes varied from a better-quality flat cap through to a boater, with bowler hats and other varieties being worn to the workplace. For those with more disposable income there would be more variety: formal suits and wing collars, waistcoats with white edging, cravats and cravat pins, and, for country wear, tweed Norfolk jackets worn with plus-fours. Dressing for dinner, in formal dinner suits, was also common in upper-class households.

From 1914 onwards, men employed at home on war service were issued with official badges that were worn with civilian dress, intended to protect them from the Order of the White Feather. Cloth armlets bearing official designations were also common; from 1915 the khaki serge armlet with red crown signified that the wearer had attested under the short-lived Derby Scheme. As the war dragged on, the number of silver war badges seen on suit lapels grew. Worn by wounded, honourably discharged soldiers and sailors, this badge was again intended to defend the wearer from the white feather. Uniforms became more commonly seen on the streets; men would return home from the front bearing the mud of

On War Service badges were introduced for civilian workers in 1914. As the war progressed, there was increasing pressure by the government to 'comb out' skilled civilians for the armed services, by the process of 'debadging'.

Silver war badge (SWB), issued to all men wounded and discharged. As with the 'On War Service' badges, the SWB was intended to protect its wearer from the white feather.

Flanders on their clothing; officers would wear their service-dress uniforms patched and reinforced like comfortable jackets.

Uniforms became de rigeur, so much so that wives and sweethearts of those serving would be photographed 'larking about' in the uniforms of their men. When the men in question returned to the front, the women – mothers, sisters, sweethearts, wives – would wear a remembrance of their men, often a simple regimental brooch, commercially produced in their thousands, or even, commonly, a badge created by the soldier from his regimental insignia. The richest examples were gold with jewels; the simplest, perhaps a button with brooch fitting.

Women's clothing, like that for men, was restricted according to class – a function of spending power and the exigencies of the working-class lifestyle. In the upper echelons, women's clothing, then as now, was directly influenced by the fashionable elite. For those with disposable income, the most desirable styles created a silhouette with a high waistline, just under the bust, echoing the 'Empire' styles of the early nineteenth century. Tunics were commonly worn over long, ankle-length skirts, worn over an underskirt of similar length. Shoes were slim in style and had a high heel, often worn with a short gaiter. Large hats were very much in evidence, with a broad brim in the early stages of the war, though shrinking to a much more manageable style by its end, matching the fashion for short, bobbed hairstyles that would continue into the post-war era.

Fashions worn by the elite were not always practical; at the outbreak of war the rich developed a penchant for the so-called 'hobble' skirt, widest at the hips and reducing to a very narrow width at the ankle. Walking any great distance in these garments was impossible; this style would not last into the more practical times of the war. Other elements of high fashion included the adoption of 'orientalism', with flowing 'harem' pantaloons and turbans. By the middle years of the war, however, dressing in high fashion was considered not to be 'the done thing', unpatriotic at a time of national emergency (and the subject of a poster campaign by

A young woman poses for the camera in summer clothes with fashionably long skirt, c. 1914. The length of women's skirts would shorten as the war progressed.

the War Savings Committee). Suits of matching jacket and skirt also became common during the war, and were worn by all who could afford them, usually set off by a hat that varied in grandeur depending on the spending power of the purchaser. For working-class women the staple of the long skirt and tunic top mirrored that of the more extravagant classes. Large hats were also in vogue, but plainer in style.

As the war developed, so did the well-to-do women's silhouette. The high waistline of the pre-war years now slipped down to a more natural position at the actual waist, and tunics lengthened to match the change. By contrast, skirts shortened, raised off the ankle to the calf, creating a much more practical daywear, and cumbersome underskirts were largely lost. Hats became much less extravagant, and colours were toned down, monochromes being more in keeping with the mood of the nation, particularly when families were mourning the loss of loved ones. Costume jewellery was also introduced at this time, an indication of the need to dress in line with wartime expectations.

With women entering the workplace in large numbers during the war, clothing became practical and utilitarian. The 'munitionettes' wore a simple wrap-around overall and a hat designed to keep their hair well out of their eyes – and well away from machinery. Distinctive

triangular 'On War Service' badges were worn with this clothing. Shoes were necessarily utilitarian, laced and low-heeled. For some occupations there was a uniform – usually with a long skirt commonly worn with a long coat, jacket and hat. Such styles were adopted for roles as diverse as bus conductresses and women police officers. Perhaps the most dramatic change was the adoption of breeches by women in some roles, in the Women's Land Army, for example.

For children, clothes more or less mirrored that of the parents, particularly for working-class children. Boys were dressed in suits, though with short trousers, and often with stiff collars and boots. Girls' dresses were more child-friendly, but again echoed those of their mothers, and were also worn with boots. Sailor suits for both sexes were common –

Children as adults – dressed up as soldiers.

and miniature military costumes made their way into the household. Postcards of children wearing these outfits are common, and in some ways a poignant reminder that the war was to touch the lives of absolutely everyone. For poorer households, choice was limited – and children wore whatever clothes were available.

By 1918, shortages of raw materials – from both the U-boat campaign and the ever-increasing demand for wool for military uniforms – meant that the supply of clothing was severely curtailed. Austerity was patriotic, and, for the rich or well off, unnecessary frills and flourishes were no longer seen on new clothes. For poorer folk, the cost of clothing had risen far beyond their means, even given the increase in disposable income enjoyed by some households; this led to the introduction of a system of standard clothing in June 1918 (the precedent for similar 'austerity' schemes re-introduced to Britain in the Second World War), whereby the textile industries were to produce materials that could be sold to produce fixed-price clothing. For men, standard suits cost between 84s and 57s 6d, overcoats were set at 63s; the children's equivalents were 45s and 35s respectively. Ever present, the War Savings Committee was to sponsor an attitude of austerity as the war came to its conclusion, which would stagger on into the peacetime world.

"YOUNG MAN, WOULD YOU MIND PUTTING A CORK IN THE SPOUT IN CASE IT GOES OFF?"

TRANSPORT

TRANSPORT had taken great strides during the Edwardian boom-time, advances that would stand Britain in good stead during the First World War. In London in particular, the idea of commuting to a place of work became a familiar reality, particularly with the increasing prevalence of buses, trams and underground railways that began in the mid-nineteenth century.

Though underground railways were relatively rare outside London (Glasgow and Liverpool being exceptions), the other transport options were repeated up and down the country. In all cases, the Victorian street scene of horse-drawn transportation would be replaced by one in which electricity, and the internal combustion engine, were dominant. The first electric tramway came to the streets of Blackpool in 1885 (the first street tram in Europe having appeared in Birkenhead in 1860), and would spread to the rest of the county, its criss-crossing overhead wires and sunken rails a common sight in many city streets. The first electric tramway in London followed in July 1901. From late 1915, there was a new circumstance. Women staff started to appear on the trams, but not without resistance in some male

Opposite:
Soldiers in full uniform and kit – and often covered with Flanders mud – were common on the nation's rail system. Donald McGill postcard.

Left: Tram tickets from south London; every opportunity was taken to persuade men to join the army.

"Doing her Bit"

FARES PLEASE.

quarters. Female tram drivers were in a minority, even as the war progressed to its conclusion, though women conductors, whose job it was to issue and check tickets, became a familiar sight across Britain from 1916. There would be some 117,000 women working in the transport industry by 1918.

Motorised omnibuses would make an appearance in Britain in 1905 and became very popular: while in 1907 only 1,205 of the 3,762 licensed buses on the streets of London were motorised, by the outbreak of war 2,908 of the 3,284 licensed buses were motor-powered. Buses and trams would carry the majority of people from their new suburbs to their places of work in the heart of the great cities – and would provide a means of servicing Britain's industrial heart with workers. In London, tens of thousands would travel by bus each day, and, just as with the tramways, the buses would be staffed by female conductors. Here, though, there would be no women drivers. This pattern would be replicated in other British cities.

'Doing her bit'. Children were popular subjects for wartime postcards, particularly children mimicking the duties of adults – in this case women bus and tram conductors.

Motor-car advert, c. 1916. There was a proliferation of car manufacturers and types available to the prospective buyer.

BUY THE

1916 *Overland*

£198

DELIVERY AT LONDON

TAKE to yourself the pleasure of the open road and study economy at the same time. Think of this: for £198 you can buy a 15-20 h.p., 4-cylinder car, beautifully finished and upholstered in real leather, with every time and temper-saving device so far invented; a car that you can learn to drive in a couple of hours. It is the 1916 "Overland."

The "Overland" stands alone as the efficient car of moderate price; it stands supreme as the car for the Owner-Driver.

ELECTRIC STARTER AND LIGHTING, MAGNETO IGNITION, AUTOMATIC OILING, THERMO-GRAVITY COOLING, ETC., ETC.

Write for the Illustrated Catalogue.

BUY OF OUR AGENTS.

WILLYS-OVERLAND Ltd.

151 Great Portland Street, London, W.

L. C. VAN BEVER, Managing Director.

Telephone : Mayfair 6700 (5 lines)   Telegrams : "Wiloreton, London."

But with crashing gears and engine noise came the crush of the private motor car. First appearing in any numbers during early Edwardian times (with the first case of manslaughter by reckless driving tried at the Old Bailey in 1906), the car would come to dominate the street scene in Britain. The Motor Car Act of 1903 raised the speed limit on Britain's city streets from 14 mph to a staggering 20 mph, and required that every driver was issued with a licence to drive by the local authorities, with the minimum driving age being set at seventeen. What was not required, however, was a driving test, though the crime of 'reckless driving' was also introduced as a counter to poor roadmanship. Motor vehicles also had to be registered, and the registration number displayed clearly upon the car. A branch of the Volunteer Training Corps – a volunteer organisation in many ways akin to the Home Guard of the Second World War –

Street scene in London, 1918, as depicted by a shoe manufacturer. Motor omnibuses and cars had long since replaced horse-drawn vehicles.

would be styled the National Motor Volunteers, and would comprise men with cars who volunteered to be of service to the nation.

With the coming of the petrol engine came the traffic jam – particularly in the years just prior to the war when there was a decided shift from the railways to the automobile. With the Model T popular on both sides of the Atlantic from 1909, a new assembly plant opened in Manchester in 1911, followed by the installation of an automated production line two years later, allowing 6,000 cars a year to be produced, each bought at a cost of £135. There were many other manufacturers. It is not surprising that, a year before the outbreak of war, it was estimated that over 90 per cent of all passenger vehicles in London were motorised. With London's streets clogged with traffic, and commuting now common, it is little wonder that there was increased demand for the underground railways during this time.

London had operated an electric underground railway since 1890 (the 'subway' in Glasgow was operated from 1896), with the opening of the City and South London Railway, and by 1900 the number of railway companies offering underground services to the capital had multiplied. The Central London Railway was opened in this year, and

The London Underground in 1908, when the independent lines were brought together in an attempt to promote the service. The distinctive 'roundel and bar' would be adopted in 1913.

with its cylindrical tunnel system had become known as the 'two-penny tube', a name that would be adopted by all 'tube' lines later. In all there would be eight independent 'tube' operators. In an effort to promote their services, the companies used the name 'Underground' from 1908, and introduced the now-familiar 'roundel and bar' logo in 1913 as the standard symbol of the combined system. In the prelude to the war, and during the war itself, the combined underground system continued to grow, electrifying lines and expanding out to the suburbs, with ever more demand for its services as the wartime population of London swelled, during the day at least.

The underground also served another purpose for the people of London; with no air-raid shelters as such, and no real coordination of 'air-raid precautions,' the arrival of the Zeppelins in 1915 and Gotha bombers in 1917 saw underground stations used for shelter, with at least 300,000 people in the city taking to the underground. This experience would be repeated in 1940 – with less approval. Elsewhere, railway viaducts, tunnels and caves would serve the same purpose.

National railways passed into state control on 4 August 1914, on the eve of war. The government had held the power to do this since 1871, and had enacted it in order to ensure the efficient transfer of men and materiel throughout Britain in the time of war. The effect of the act was 'to coordinate the demands of the railways of the civil community with those necessary to meet the special requirements of the naval and military authorities'. With 120 rail-operating companies across Britain, this was very necessary. The movement of rail freight and passengers passed to the War Railway Council, staffed by military representatives and members of the Board of Trade. There were a large number of 'special' trains – mostly carrying troops. The longest was soon nicknamed 'The Misery'. Carrying naval personnel from London to Thurso (in order to man the Grand Fleet at Scapa Flow), the journey was some 728 miles and took over twenty-two hours.

Rail stations were scenes of great activity and heartbreak. Troop trains from the south coast into the London termini would be packed with soldiers returning on leave, their uniforms begrimed with mud from the trenches, their weapons and equipment stowed in luggage racks. Trains would arrive bearing severely wounded soldiers en route to hospitals, their off-loading a flurry of activity with nurses and medical staff. Departing trains would be bearing men back to France, their loved ones suffering the agony of parting. In the midst of all this, private passengers could travel, but the opportunity for them to do so was severely curtailed – particularly as cheap tickets were withdrawn in spring 1915. Rail companies now no longer 'touted for business'; the railways were on a war footing.

With the rail system dominated by the transport of men and materiel throughout the country, it was perhaps inevitable that the system – and its operators – would be pushed to breaking point. Perhaps because of these circumstances, the worst rail disaster in British history was to occur on 22 May 1915 near Gretna Green in Scotland. This crash took place at a busy junction with sidings at Qunitinshill, and involved five trains. A signalman had shunted a local train onto the 'up' line in order to let two express trains pass on the 'down' line; a troop train ran into the waiting local train and one of the express trains also ran into the wreckage. The wooden-framed and -panelled gas-lit carriages of the troop train were engulfed by fire. The crash caused the deaths of 226 people – most of them soldiers of the 7th Battalion Royal Scots on their way to the Dardanelles – with some 246 others injured. Of the 500-strong battalion, just fifty-seven men were present at roll call that afternoon.

Engine from the London and North Western Railway in the pre-war period. The LNWR considered itself to be the most important of all railway lines during the period, and served all the major industrial cities of late Edwardian Britain. It would fall under War Office control during the war.

FOUR CYLINDER COMPOUND ENGINE "LA FRANCE."
BUILT IN MARCH 1900.

TOMMY

Sung by
MISS
GOODIE
REEVE

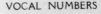

'ullo!

Bruce Bairnsfather

CHARLES B. COCHRAN'S
PRODUCTION

The Better 'Ole

OR THE ROMANCE OF "OLD BILL"

By BRUCE BAIRNSFATHER & ARTHUR ELIOT
Music by HERMAN DAREWSKI

2/- NET

HERMAN DAREWSKI MUSIC PUBLISHING CO.
(ST. SWITHIN'S SYNDICATE LTD.)
142, Charing Cross Road, London, W.C.2

AMERICA: LEO FEIST, INC., NEW YORK.   PRINTED IN ENGLAND   Copyright, MCMXVII, by Herman Darewski Music Publishing Co.

RELAXATION AND ENTERTAINMENT

MUSIC HALL was the dominant aspect of entertainment in Edwardian life – an aspect that would continue well into the Great War – though, like many other threads of the social fabric of Britain, it would go into decline in the post-war world. With its origins in saloon bars in public houses of the early Victorian period, the music hall developed into a variety theatre that gained in both popular standing and respectability during the latter part of the Victorian era, becoming a high art in the reign of Edward VII. By the outbreak of the First World War, the music hall was a popular mass-entertainment venue – its stars household names. Most major towns and cities boasted large theatres catering for the galaxy of stars who toured the country. Though many of these buildings survive today in other guises, most have fallen foul of the years. The largely forgotten stars included the impersonator Harry Tate, comedian George Robey, risqué singer Marie Lloyd, and the acrobatic Little Tich – with his long 'slap' shoes.

For some commentators, music hall reached the peak of its popularity during the Great War, especially as increasing numbers of servicemen – particularly officers with some disposable income – sought escape from the trials of the trenches whilst home on leave. With the glamour of the musical hall came the clamour to use it as a recruiting platform, and among the many who joined the plea for more men to join up was the male impersonator Vesta Tilley. Born Matilda Alice Pownes in 1864, she was to become famous for the recruitment drives she organised. Tilley was extraordinarily successful, dressing in a variety of uniforms to put her point across and earning the nickname 'Britain's best recruiting sergeant'. Performing songs such as 'Jolly good luck to the girl who loves a soldier', her act evolved as the war progressed, with the addition of the song 'I've got a bit of a Blighty one' – a reference to a wound that would get a soldier away from the front, and back home to 'Blighty'.

Opposite: 'Tommy', a song from the musical revue, *The Better 'Ole*, which opened at the Oxford Theatre in London in 1917.

Musical theatre, with slightly more pretention, would also be popular, with many revues of the day carrying patriotic slogans and songs throughout the war. But with casualties increasing, the nation would have little stomach for such sentiments as the war progressed, and they would be toned down. Typical of these shows was the musical revue, with *Chu Chin Chow* (which premiered in 1916 and ran for five years) and *The Bing Boys are Here* (adopted by the soldiers of 1918 led by General Byng) proving popular. *Chu Chin Chow* was particularly favoured with soldiers on leave – reputedly for its chorus of 'slave girls' who appeared to be scantily clad. *The Bing Boys are Here* also opened in 1916 (starring George Robey), and included the hit song 'If you were the only boy in the world', which had a poignant resonance for many at the time. There were many others – including *The Better 'Ole – Or the Romance of 'Old Bill'*, which opened at the Oxford Theatre in 1917, based on Bruce Bairnsfather's popular soldier figure and old lag Old Bill.

Vesta Tilley, 'Britain's best recruiting sergeant', and music-hall star. A male impersonator, she dressed up in a variety of military uniforms during the war.

One of the most important outputs from musical theatre was sheet music. With few music-hall singers making gramophone records at the time, the sale of sheet music guaranteed that the songs most associated with them would be played at home – especially since cheap pianos had appeared on the market prior to the Great War (though most of them made in Germany). The song 'It's a long way to Tipperary' was made popular through the sale of sheet music in pre-war years. By the end of 1914, adopted as a soldier's song and loaded with sentiment, the song sheet was selling a staggering 100,000 copies a year. Nevertheless, records and gramophones became popular during the war, particularly

Sheet music from the wartime hit *Chu Chin Chow*, famed for its chorus of slave girls – and popular with soldiers on leave for the same reason.

"IT'S A LONG, LONG WAY FROM TIPPERARY."

MARCHING THROUGH BERLIN.—The Kaiser Wilhelm Strasse.
Paddy wrote a letter to his Irish Molly O',
Saying, "Should you not receive it, write and let me know!
If I make mistakes in 'spelling,' Molly, dear," said he,
"Remember it's the pen that's bad, don't lay the blame on me.'
"It's a long way to Tipperary, it's a long way to go;
It's a long way to Tipperary, to the sweetest girl I know!
Good-bye Piccadilly, farewell Leicester Square,
It's a long, long way to Tipperary, but my heart's right there!
By permission of B. Feldman & Co., 2 & 3 Arthur St., London, W.C.

Soldiers want Music wherever they go.

SEND HIM

DECCA

THE PORTABLE GRAMOPHONE

Weighs only 13 lbs., can be carried easily from place to place, yet as powerful and rich in tone and as clear in reproduction as the largest gramophone made. When closed, looks like a handbag; when open, is immediately ready to play without tiresome preliminaries. Takes any make and size of needle record. The best present you can send to any soldier—Officer or Private.

| In Leather-Cloth Case £2 10 0 | Compressed Fibre Case £3 10 0 | Solid Cowhide Case £5 15 0 |

Of Harrods, Army and Navy Stores, Whiteley's, and all leading Stores and Music Dealers.
Descriptive pamphlet and name of nearest agent free on application to the Manufacturers:

THE DULCEPHONE CO.,
32-34 WORSHIP STREET, LONDON, E.C.

Illustrated Descriptive Folder FREE Send for a Copy.

when the unwieldy horn was incorporated within the body of the machine. This made it portable, and 'trench gramophones', manufactured by Decca in 1915, were popular with officers. Patriotic tunes such as 'Keep the home fires burning', 'Take me back to dear old Blighty' and 'Roses of no-man's land' were played at the time, and still have power to move today; other records, such as a recording of a gas attack at the front, would perhaps have more specialist appeal. With music all the rage, so came dancing. Dancing clubs, such as they were, were more the preserve of the moneyed classes, and saw the introduction of such dance crazes as the foxtrot, introduced in 1914 as a reaction to ragtime music.

The only real threat to music hall was the advent of the cinema. The first purpose-built cinema in Britain had opened in 1907; slow to take off, the medium gathered in momentum such that, by 1912, there were 4,000 dedicated cinemas up and down the country. Perceived at first as a low form of entertainment, the acceptance of film as art took some time. With the British film industry slow to start, around 90 per cent of all films shown during the war were derived from America – and a board of censors set to work to ensure that these were suitable for British eyes. The cinema stars of the time included Charlie Chaplin, who

Above left:
'It's a long way to Tipperary', the 'most famous song of the war'. Numerous postcards were produced to celebrate it. The song was mercilessly parodied.

Above:
Decca 'trench gramophone', 1915. Portable gramophones could be carried into the trenches – or equally, they could be used at home.

Charlie Chaplin became an international star. From humble beginnings, his move to America led him to star in his own films throughout the war. Popular with all, his image was used in many wartime situations, such as this comic from 1915.

was a hit in the land of his birth, as well as in his adopted country. His on-screen persona, the Tramp, would appear early on in 1914, in the short *Kid Auto Races at Venice*; he would feature again in a large number of films that appeared during the First World War period, including *Shoulder Arms*, produced in October 1918, in which a uniformed Tramp appears in France. Chaplin's image would be used widely. But there were hit films in other genres: romances, westerns (with Tom Mix in starring role), and any other type in which escapism was possible.

However, in some circles, the cinema was viewed with suspicion; after all, it involved a darkened venue, and as young women were no longer chaperoned, the moralists of the day were concerned about

the well-being of girls who accompanied soldiers to the 'flicks'. Whether soldiers would be willing to accompany their sweethearts to the film *The Battle of the Somme* when it opened in August 1916 is another matter. Shot by official cinematographers Geoffrey Malins and John McDowell, the film was the first to depict trench warfare. Using a combination of staged shots and actual battle sequences, the film showed not only the might of modern warfare but also poignant scenes of British and German casualties, bringing the horror of the war home to British audiences. It was a huge success, with twenty million tickets sold in the first six weeks of its release. Cinema would not be the same again.

Sport had become mass entertainment during the latter part of the nineteenth century, particularly since the Football Association had created the concept of the professional player, and aligned over twenty clubs to play each other regularly in two leagues. Not only was it a spectator sport – drawing huge crowds – it was also a participation sport, with amateur clubs springing up from a wide variety of organisations from church groups to industrial clubs. But with the Football Association representing professional clubs, the sport became beleaguered by campaigners who sought to turn both the spectators and the players into soldiers. Players were assaulted by messages to abandon their careers, from sandwich boards to cartoons in *Punch*. Many men did join – some forming Kitchener's Army battalions, like the 23rd Royal Fusiliers (1st Sportsmen's) and the 17th Middlesex Regiment (1st Football). The professional game held on until spring 1915, when it finally bowed to pressure, being abandoned – along with most other spectator sports – for 'the duration'.

Amateur football team in the pre-war period. Football would continue in popularity throughout the war, though the professional game would be suspended in 1915.

A Mancunian soldier enjoys a beer with his civilian drinking friends, c. 1915. Drinking time would be curtailed during the war under the Defence of the Realm Act.

Drinking was a popular pastime for all ages, but was one that would be severely curtailed during the war. 'Taking the pledge' meant abstinence from alcoholic drink, a concept of earlier, moralising times. The country at war, concerns were high that the loss of working days through drink could have an adverse effect on the wartime economy. With the chancellor of the Exchequer, David Lloyd George (a Welsh Nonconformist), prepared to wage war on the 'enemy' that was drink, it was not surprising that under the Defence of the Realm Act in 1914 licensing hours were reined in, such that pubs were forced to close at 12.30 a.m. in London, and considerably earlier elsewhere. By the end of the first year of the war the closing time would have been moved back to 11 p.m. Lloyd George also ensured that the price of drink increased (a pint of beer increasing from 3d to 4d in the first budget of the war, and rising steadily to a set price of around 5d in 1918), and decreased the potency of beer by 'watering down' in 1916. Furthermore Lloyd George persuaded the king to show leadership by 'taking the pledge' to abstain from alcohol in 1915. So-called 'treating', the buying of rounds of drinks, was also outlawed. By the end of the war, not surprisingly, convictions for drunkenness had fallen dramatically, from an average weekly rate of 3,388 for England and Wales in 1914, to just 449 in 1918.

Women workers joined their male colleagues at the bar during this period; their hard labour warranted refreshment just the same as with men. Though this was frowned upon initially, objections could hardly stand given their commitment to the war effort. All would join in the celebrations, subdued at first, at the signing of the armistice with Germany on 11 November 1918, and the more substantial Victory celebration that would follow in the wake of peace negotiations, on 19 July 1919, billed 'the greatest day in the whole world'.

The armistice was followed by the peace celebrations of 19 July 1919; the 'greatest day in the whole world' would be marred by the influenza pandemic.

EDUCATION AND SOCIAL SERVICE

THE RETURN of the Liberals to power in 1906 saw the development of some policies that would later pave the way for the construction of a proto-welfare state, paid for through increased taxation. Given that most of the country's workforce was paid below the tax threshold of £160 per year, the tax burden fell on the middle and upper classes. This was not without opposition; on the other side of the House, the Conservatives mounted a fierce attack on the reforms, going so far as to use their majority to vote down the so-called 'People's Budget' of 1909 in the House of Lords. The government did not lie down – a direct result of this defeat was the first curb on the power of the Lords, with the passing of the Parliament Act of 1911, which ensured that the House of Commons would have its way.

The reforming agenda of the Liberal government of 1906 was driven by the findings of two influential reports on the health of the nation compiled by Charles Booth (who drew up a series of poverty maps for London, 1886–1903) and Seebohm Rowntree (who studied working-class life in York, and published his influential book, *Poverty, A Study of Town Life*, in 1901). Both men recognised that, in the late nineteenth century, at least 30 per cent of urban populations were living in poverty and had no means of escaping its clutches. Unemployment, illness and old age were the most significant factors. The Liberals were committed to the fact that it was no longer sufficient to sit back and take a laissez-faire approach to government – there needed to be an active involvement in improving the lot of the average citizen, with special attention to the young, the old, the sick and the unemployed.

One of the first of the Liberals' progressive policies was to allow local authorities to provide two free meals a day for poor schoolchildren under the Education (Provision of Meals) Act; the provision of these was made compulsory by law in 1914, when

Opposite:
A mother baths her baby in the kitchen, c. 1914. In robust health, and from a reasonably well-off family, this child will prosper. Poor circumstances and inadequate nutrition would be the reality for many wartime families.

fourteen million meals would be provided. Intended to combat poverty and malnutrition in children, it was shockingly effective; research showed that during school holiday periods, the health and nutrition of many children from poor backgrounds declined markedly, with growth and body weight both falling off. A year after the introduction of free meals came school medical inspections, which quickly identified health problems, but did little or nothing to cure them. This would have to wait until the institution of free medical treatment for schoolchildren in 1912 – a result of the coalition government formed with Labour MPs – when grants were made to local authorities to provide healthcare. By the outbreak of war, two-thirds of education authorities were providing medical treatment for their pupils.

National Insurance Act certificate, 1916. Unemployment benefits would only be paid to those in a few trades; these would increase during the war.

If problems with the health and well-being of schoolchildren were a priority, so was the poverty of old age. With no government provision, elderly people had to rely on their families to support them; so in 1908 the Liberal government introduced the Old Age Pension Act, legislation that would see the first old-age pensions become law in 1909. By 1914, one million people were in receipt of a pension. These pensions were paid at a rate of 5s per week to single people over seventy with an annual income of less than £21, while a married couple received 7s 6d a week, to be collected from the Post Office. Smaller amounts were paid to higher earners, and those with an annual income of £31 10s or more received no pension at all. With life expectancy low amongst the elderly poor, many died long before they were old enough to qualify for a pension; and those who lived to claim it found that the amount was little enough to keep them well.

Sickness was a major factor in keeping people in poverty, yet it was plain that the poor could not afford medical support. The National Insurance Act was introduced in 1911 in order to alleviate this issue. It provided health insurance for all those

The Prince of Wales was the patron of several war relief charities in 1914, raising money for both Belgian refugees and those challenged by hardship at home.

earning less than £160 per year (the tax threshold) – which was most of the working population. Workers were expected to contribute 4d a week, and this was matched by contributions of 3d from the employers and 2d from the state. In return, workers were provided with a sickness benefit entitlement of 9s, free medical treatment and maternity benefit of 30s. Unemployment benefits provided by the act were much more restricted – and applied only to those who worked in the building industry, or who were employed in the iron and steel trades, and ship building – seven trades in all. This meant that it applied to just two and a quarter million men; the benefits were fixed to these trades as these were often affected by market fluctuations in the pre-war period. These men were given 7s unemployment benefit a week for a maximum of fifteen weeks in any year if they became unemployed. The number of trades covered under the act would swell during the war – reflecting the increased number of trades and war workers.

Above: Paper flags like these were a produced in their millions, and for numerous causes. These are for the support of wounded soldiers.

Families were assailed by multiple claims on their limited resources during the war. Charities in particular seemed to proliferate, with many people giving their time to collect money for the diverse causes that clamoured for attention during the 'flag days' that became so prevalent. There was the National Relief Fund, supported by the Prince of Wales, which was intended to alleviate economic hardships. And with a flood of Belgians arriving on British shores in 1914 (totalling a quarter of a million people), there was an obvious need to feed and house them. Fashionable society ladies vied to house the most 'suitable' refugees, and there was concern that all comers should be housed and fed. The War Refugees Committee was set up on 24 August 1914 to support the people of 'gallant little Belgium', the victims of atrocities perpetrated across the country by the invading Germans. Yet, by 1915, the strain of welcoming some of the guests of 'plucky little Belgium' was starting to show.

Below: Flag sellers in south London, c. 1916. Charity flags became a phenomenon of the war.

There were other calls on the family purse, particularly the provision of 'comforts' for the troops at the front. Cigarettes and tobacco were particularly prized. Famously, the *Weekly Despatch* newspaper organised a tobacco fund for the troops and Bert Thomas's famous drawings, 'Arf a "mo"

Above: Certificates given by the Overseas Club to schoolchildren for raising money for soldiers' 'comforts'.

Below: Conway Street Elementary School, Birkenhead, in north-west England. A grand Victorian building built for the Birkenhead School Board in 1893, it was transferred to the Local Education Committee in 1902 under the School Act.

Kaiser!', were used as a means of drumming up support for it. In school, children were encouraged by the Overseas Club to bring coppers into school on specific days in the year in order to collect for comforts for men at the front; they were rewarded with certificates.

In the early part of the twentieth century, the standard of education in the United Kingdom was lagging seriously behind that elsewhere in Europe, and increasingly the United States, which had created secondary, publically funded high schools in the years before the war. Along with the expectation that this would create a well-educated workforce in Britain's economic rivals was the recognition that the British system, and in particular that operated within England and Wales, was becoming outdated. A central plank of the new Conservative government of 1902 was the view that this could no longer be allowed to continue. The arguments made by Prime Minister Arthur Balfour were cogently put: Britain could not afford to lag behind its continental rivals in the provision of an educated workforce. The 1902 School Act created local education authorities (LEAs) based on local authorities. Each LEA had control of religious schools, insisting that no pupil be forced to conform to religious ritual. This development was fiercely resisted by the Catholic Church, which, as late as 1917, issued an edict that Catholic parents would be in danger of excommunication if they sent their children to non-Catholic schools.

The 1902 act also laid the foundations for the expansion of the system of secondary schools, large numbers of which were built in the period before the First World War. The Liberal government of 1906 continued and expanded the work of its predecessors. Under the Liberals, poorer children showing promise at elementary schools were able to go on into secondary education. Despite this, and even though a quarter of the places in secondary schools were free, in 1914 the population of these higher schools stood at just 200,000, with most pupils leaving education by fourteen, and many more leaving before then. In early days it was the poverty of the families that dictated this; later in the war, there was the draw of earning a decent wage in the munitions factories. In fact, it is thought that in 1917 as many as 600,000 children left education early to take up employment. It was not until August 1918 that a school-leaving age of fourteen was set as a minimum mandatory requirement, as part of the new Education Act that set out the suspended Liberal agenda for a national school system.

It was the desire of the Liberal government to draw up a national education system, but this was largely shelved in 1914; pressures of the war meant that children were also in demand to take their place within the workplace, particularly where it was to boost the war effort, and was therefore in the 'national interest'. In this way, at least 600,000 children were put to work before fulfilling their school commitments; the figure may well have been much higher.

Though attendance at school was mandatory, it remained a concern; so much so that some education authorities instigated certificates and even medals to reward good examples. Those issued by London County Council were the most complex, and even received royal assent. The King's Medal (previously the King Edward VII medal) was awarded to children by the London School Board – and later the LCC – for 'regular and punctual attendance'; in practice this meant 100 per cent attendance. Pupils had to earn 'tickets' for a week of good attendance, which were exchanged for a reward card for a full term's attendance. A full set of reward cards earned the pupil a medal. A pupil was eligible to receive one medal every year, building up to a silver medal if the full seven years' attendance was to the required standard. These are rare indeed. Though the medal continued to be awarded until 1915, in the latter part of the war, with materials scarce, it was replaced by a certificate, then reinstated briefly for 1919–20.

London County Council Certificate for good school attendance, 1917–18. Such certificates were awarded to those who could afford to attend school. Many children were tempted away early by the promise of good wages during the war.

The King's Medal, granted to children in London for attendance and other good conduct. From 1916 onwards, it was replaced by a certificate.

HEALTH

THE TRANSITION from the Victorian to the Edwardian (and early 'Georgian') periods could not have been more startling in terms of the improvement in public health. With the vast majority of the population on a low wage, and with housing stock often crowded and insanitary, figures of infant mortality and deaths from common diseases were high until just before the First World War, when they plummeted. The positive effects of the Liberal government's social agenda were to pay dividends. By the outbreak of war, infant mortality had fallen by 38 per cent, while the death rates for measles, scarlet fever, whooping cough and tuberculosis had also fallen dramatically to around half that experienced in Victorian Britain. Improvements in sanitary conditions and housing in the Edwardian era had greatly improved the health of the nation. These diseases were still prevalent, however, particularly amongst the poor, but their impact was much reduced.

This phenomenon would continue for the home population during the First World War. In fact, social historians have long puzzled over the fact that one of the most destructive wars in British history appears to have led to improvements in life expectancy on the home front. Their findings demonstrate that, unlike the reason of improved diet during the Second World War, the health gains in the First World War were simply down to the fact that the average citizen had more income from war work – and therefore more money to spend on the necessities of life such as food. Ironically enough, access to doctors was also much reduced during the war – as many as half of all medical staff were away serving with the military medical services throughout the war. Most of the killer diseases – tuberculosis and other respiratory conditions, and transmittable diseases such as measles and whooping cough – had no cure as such, and the sufferer simply had to wait for the disease to abate. There was little that doctors could do, except promote greater hygiene practices. There was a resurgence of tuberculosis in

Opposite:
Voluntary Aid
Detachment
(VAD) volunteer
nurses served
both at home
and overseas.

Right:
Tuberculosis remained a killer throughout the war. TB wards like this one relied on the power of fresh air. It was a faint hope.

Below: Middle-class mother and child, c. 1913. Infant mortality rates were of concern in late Victorian Britain, but had fallen dramatically with the advent of the Liberal government's social-care policies. This continued during the war.

the early part of the war but numbers of cases soon fell back into line with the previous trend of decline. It would be the influenza pandemic of 1918–19 that would skew mortality figures at the end of conflict. Infant mortality rates would decline throughout the war, with much concentration on the support of midwives by the government.

With the majority of the population of Britain on a low income at the outbreak of war (80 per cent of the country being working class, many of them close to poverty), ensuring that families received an adequate supply of nutritious foods was less an issue of wartime restrictions, and more of being able to afford food at all. Parallels with the home front during the Second World War are therefore pretty much false. Many people were undernourished and as a consequence undersized. The concept of a balanced diet was not prevalent: the now-familiar vitamin complexes had only been discovered – and named – by medical scientists just prior to the war. Knowledge of nutrition was limited. The introduction of free school meals for the poorest children, and the other policies of the pre-war Liberal reform agenda, had helped improve the health of the nation, yet there was a long way to go. The food queues, shortages and rationing of the First World War did little to improve the lot of the average citizen, yet overall the health of the nation did improve during the war. Death from diarrhoeal diseases, a function of poor food hygiene and quality, would show a marked decline year-on-year through the war years.

A war hospital in Britain. Many of these would be set up in large houses and grand buildings across the country.

Though the health of the average citizen improved, there was constant evidence on the streets of Britain of the war being fought overseas, with the wounded and maimed released from military service, or recovering. With home leave a barely hoped-for luxury in the First World War, it is not surprising that the common soldier wished for a simple wound or debilitating illness that would take him out of the front line, and home to the green fields of Britain. Such wounds became known as 'Blighty' or 'cushy' wounds, sufficiently serious to be sent home on a hospital ship, sufficiently slight so as not to be life-threatening or permanently debilitating.

Princess Mary as a VAD.

There was a general feeling of goodwill towards wounded heroes that persisted throughout the war; crowds would often gather to greet them at the main railway termini. War hospitals up and down the country received soldiers 'from the front'. Set up in large private houses and municipal buildings in order to satisfy the demand for suitable accommodation, they were often staffed by 'VADs', volunteer nurses belonging to the Voluntary Aid Detachments. The VADs were originally founded in 1909 by the War Office, the British Red Cross and the Order of St John to provide support to the Territorial Army medical service. With the outbreak of war in 1914 there would be floods of volunteers, not all of them suited to medical work, many with little or no experience.

"POOR FELLOW——WERE YOU
WOUNDED IN THE GREAT PUSH?"
"NO MUM! IN THE LITTLE MARY."

Hospital blues.
This distinctive
blue uniform
would be seen
up and down
the country
throughout
the war.

Some 38,000 VADs would work in hospitals up and down the country while others would serve overseas. Not only were there wounded soldiers to nurse, but the ailments of a beleaguered nation also had to be supported. VADs worked some three thousand military auxiliary hospitals and convalescent homes during the war, supporting those soldiers sent home to Blighty. Soldiers sent to hospital were ordered out of their familiar khaki and into hospital blue, a simple suit of blue clothes worn with a distinctive red tie. Although a poor fit, hospital blues provided a distinctive sign of a wounded soldier's status, a badge of honour that distinguished him as a man from the front.

One of the many tragedies of the Great War was the influenza pandemic which blighted the world just as the war was drawing to its conclusion in 1918. Incorrectly labelled 'Spanish flu' at the time (based on a misconception of the severity of the disease in this neutral county), the actual source and origin of the influenza outbreak is still debated. Many link it to large concentrations of troops, such as the massive British Etaples training camp near Le Touquet in France. Certainly the cramped living quarters of the men, and their relatively poor diet, may well have had a role in its spread – as did their movement overseas. The impact of the virus was felt everywhere, with many communities blighted. Chemists' shops tried to peddle remedies and immunities – but these were to no avail.

The pandemic spread rapidly across the world, claiming as its victims many otherwise healthy adults, many of whom had come through the war unharmed. With this strain of influenza virus causing the body's immune system to over-react, this demographic would be the hardest hit, as the young and old have weaker immune systems. For soldiers to lose their lives from a case of the 'flu' in this way was a sad irony. The influenza came in waves, lasting from June 1918 through to the end of 1920, killing up to one hundred million people worldwide; five hundred million were infected. It was a tragic, ironic conclusion to a terrible war.

PLACES TO VISIT

Beamish, Beamish, County Durham DH9 0RG. Tel. 0191 370 4000.
Victorian/Edwardian living history museum.

Black Country Museum, Tipton Road, Dudley DY1 4SQ. Tel. 0121 5579643.
Victorian/Edwardian living history museum.

Geffrye Museum, 136 Kingsland Road, London E2 8EA. Tel. 0207 7399893.
Museum of interiors.

Imperial War Museum London, Lambeth Road, SE1 6HZ. Tel. 0207
4165000.

Imperial War Museum North, The Quays, Trafford Wharf Road, Trafford
Park Manchester M17 1T. Tel. 01618 364000.

Museum of Brands, Packaging and Advertising, 2 Colville Mews, Lonsdale
Road, Notting Hill, London W11 2AR. Tel. 0207 9080880.

Royal Gunpowder Mills, Beaulieu Drive, Waltham Abbey, Essex EN9 1J.
Tel. 01992 707370.
Former ordnance factory.

PLACES

Cleopatra's Needle, Victoria Embankment, London.
Zeppelin damage to ancient monument.

Port Sunlight Museum and Garden Village, 23 King George's Drive, Port
Sunlight, Wirral CH62 5DX. Tel. 01516 446466.
Classic garden village, constructed by Lord Lever.

Woolwich Arsenal, Woolwich, London SE18 6ST.
Site of former Royal Arsenal, now home to the Royal Artillery Museum.

MEMORIALS

Ashford tank, St George's Square, Ashford, Kent.
Last surviving Great War presentation tank.

Chilwell Memorial, St Mary Magdalene Church, Attenborough,
Nottinghamshire NG9 6AS.
Memorial to the National Filling Factory explosion, 1918.

Cuffley Memorial, Cuffley, Hertfordshire.
Monument to Lieutenant W. Leefe Robinson's attack on the SL11 airship.

Postman's Park, Little Britain, London.
Memorial to Heroic Self Sacrifice, which includes two Great War police
memorials, one associated with Silvertown.

Poplar Children's memorial, Poplar Recreation Ground, East India Dock
Road, Poplar, London E14.
Memorial to the children from North Street School killed by a raid in 1917.

Rosebank Cemetery, 104 Pilrig Street, Edinburgh EH6 5BB.
Quintinshill railway disaster memorial.

Silvertown Memorial, North Woolwich Road, Silvertown, London E16.
Silvertown factory explosion, 1917.

INDEX